SOME
ANCIENT NOVELS

LEUCIPPE AND CLITOPHON
DAPHNIS AND CHLOE
THE SATIRICON
THE GOLDEN ASS

By

F. A. TODD

PROFESSOR OF LATIN IN THE
UNIVERSITY OF SYDNEY

Essay Index Reprint Series

BOOKS FOR LIBRARIES PRESS
FREEPORT, NEW YORK

First published 1940
Reprinted 1968

LIBRARY OF CONGRESS CATALOG CARD NUMBER:
68-29250

PRINTED IN THE UNITED STATES OF AMERICA

PREFACE

T HE lectures contained in this little book were delivered, in their original form, by invitation of the Sydney University Extension Board, before an audience which consisted mainly of members of the University. They are quite unpretentious. I hope, of course, that the expert who may happen to read them will find in them, now and again, something more palatable and wholesome than *crambe repetita*; but they will fulfil their chief purpose if, without undue parade of technicalities, they provide the 'general reader', and the student whose Greek and Latin studies are not likely to have led him to the originals, with trustworthy guidance in the endeavour to learn what the Novel was like in its remote beginnings. That they appear now in the solemnity of print is due to requests, which I could not be so ungracious as to refuse, that came both from the Board and from colleagues and others who had done me the honour of hearing them. In revising them for this wider publication I have made no essential change of form, but have eliminated a few references to the particular audience, made some additions and corrections in the light of new knowledge and further thought, and appended a considerable number of short footnotes. Throughout the book, with only one or two exceptions, I have given to Greek names the Latin forms in which they are most likely to be encountered in English literature.

My cordial thanks, for much help and encouragement of various kinds, are due, and gladly offered, to the Vice-Chancellor of Sydney University (Dr. R. S. Wallace); the Sydney University Extension Board;

Professor A. W. Boase and Mr. Ritchie Girvan, of Glasgow University; Professor W. L. Renwick, of King's College, University of Newcastle; Professor A. R. Chisholm, of Melbourne University; and, among colleagues in the University of Sydney, Emeritus Professor Sir Mungo MacCallum, Professor E. R. Holme, Mr. R. G. Howarth, Mr. A. H. Robinson, and Mr. G. P. Shipp. Mr. Shipp did me the great service of reading the book in manuscript and offering valuable suggestions.

F. A. T.

UNIVERSITY OF SYDNEY,
April 1939

ERRATA

Page 99, line 25, *for* Things go so fast
read Things go fast

Pages vi, line 1, and 49, footnote
for Prof. A. W. Boase
read Prof. A. M. Boase

CONTENTS

I

'LEUCIPPE AND CLITOPHON'

LIST OF CHIEF CHARACTERS

CALLI'GONE: daughter of Hippias and half-sister of Clitophon

CALLI'STHENES: a young Byzantine

CHAE'REAS: an Egyptian

CHAR'MIDES: an Egyptian general

CLI'NIAS: a young Tyrian, cousin of Clitophon

CLI'O: maid to Leucippe

CLI'TOPHŌN: son of Hippias and half-brother of Calligone

CŌ'NŌPS: slave to Panthea

GOR'GIAS: an Egyptian

HIP'PIAS: a Tyrian, father of Clitophon and Calligone

LACAE'NA: a name assumed by Leucippe

LEUCIP'PE: daughter of Sostratus and Panthea

MELIT'TE: an Ephesian woman, wife of Thersander

MENELA'US: an Egyptian

PANTHE'A: wife of Sostratus and mother of Leucippe

PRIEST OF AR'TEMIS ('Diana of the Ephesians')

SA'TYRUS: a slave, servant to Clitophon

SŌ'STHENES: steward to Thersander

SŌ'STRATUS: a Byzantine, half-brother of Hippias and father of Leucippe

THERSAN'DER: an Ephesian, husband of Melitte

SOME nine centuries ago the eminent Michael Psellos gave advice to the studious person who would enter upon his novitiate in Greek. 'Don't begin', he said, 'with the *Leucippe and Clitophon* and the *Daphnis and Chloe*, but read first the more serious works of the great age of Greek literature.' Here, incidentally, is striking proof, if proof were needed, that those two romances, and presumably others also, were still popular, in the Byzantine world, far on in the Middle Ages, seven centuries and more after they were written. The advice, for those to whom it was addressed, was sound, for it is not to be denied that in the novel Greek literature falls far short of its best; but we moderns, while agreeing with Psellos in his estimate of relative values, have a special reason for turning our attention not only to the two romances which he named but also to the

B

ancient novels generally, both the Greek and the Latin. For the novel has now become the dominant form of literature, and the ancient novel, even apart from its intrinsic merits, claims the respectful notice that is due to the ancestor of a numerous and distinguished progeny. The purpose of these lectures, however, is less to trace literary genealogies than to show, by description and criticism of typical examples, what Greek and Latin novels were like.

Of the four novels chosen for extended treatment, two are Greek and two are Latin. The *Leucippe and Clitophon* of Achilles Tatius dates, it seems, from the third century after Christ and is a typical representative of by far the largest class of ancient novels, the tale of love and adventure. The *Daphnis and Chloe* of Longus, somewhat earlier in date, contains some of the ingredients of this class, but stands alone in ancient literature as a union of the Romance with the Pastoral. My two Latin examples are a little older. The *Satiricon* of Petronius, written by a distinguished member of Nero's court in the middle of the first century after Christ, is a work of real genius, showing little or no trace of Greek influence in any essential, which tells, with satirical humour, a tale of rogues and the vulgar rich. Finally, the *Metamorphoses* of Apuleius, commonly known as *The Golden Ass*, belongs to the second half of the second century after Christ and narrates the adventures of a man who, too curious in magic, was changed into a donkey. In it is embedded that jewel among fairy-tales *Cupid and Psyche*.

Among the Greeks, poetic fiction is as old as Homer, and throughout the long history of their literature there is no age that does not furnish examples, in epic, or drama, or pastoral, or whatever other form it may assume. The comparatively late emergence of prose fiction into Greek literature was therefore not due to any distaste for fiction as such, but points to the persistence, long after Greek prose had attained its full development, of the feeling that verse is the proper vehicle for works of the imagination. This same feeling, I believe, rather than mere respect for tradition, explains why the Greeks, though they invented the prose dialogue as a literary form, retained verse as the medium for drama of every kind to the very end.

Prose fiction makes its first appearance in History, from which indeed, the cynic will say, it has never since been expelled. Herodotus, born about 485 B.C., was not only 'the Father of History' but also, nearly twenty-four centuries before Mr. Phillips Oppenheim, 'the Prince of Story-tellers'; and in his work are tales, admirably told, about Gyges and Candaules and Croesus and the rest, which, whether wholly or in part, are fiction: and fiction, be it noted, which bears the marks of Oriental origin. Xenophon, less than half a century later, carries us a step farther, exhibiting in his *Cyro-paedia* or *Education of Cyrus* a blend of history and fiction, one episode in which, the romantic love and adventures of Abradatas and Panthea, anticipates in its chief characteristics the full-length novels of later times. Here also you will note the Eastern origin of the story.

The time of the novel was not yet come, but meanwhile the taste for the short story, and especially for the kind of short story which we call by the Italian name *novella*, was growing. Large numbers of these, whether indigenous or derived from Eastern sources, were current in the Greek cities of Asia Minor, and in due course were collected and reduced to writing. Of the most famous of them, the *Milesian Tales*, I shall have something to say in a later lecture. Slight in themselves, and often far from respectable, they exercised a considerable influence both on the ancient romance and on later European literature. In the latter half of the first century before Christ, Parthenius, the minor poet who is said to have had the distinction of teaching Virgil Greek, wrote in prose a large number of short mythological love-stories to furnish his friend the Roman poet Cornelius Gallus with material for elegiac poems. Of these stories thirty-six are extant. They are not novels, nor are they *novelle* in the ordinary use of that term; but if they were divorced from mythology and related of invented persons, 'almost all', as Sir Stephen Gaselee[1] remarks, 'might serve as the plots for novels, or rather parts of novels, of the kind' which we are about to consider.

To the time of Parthenius, or perhaps somewhat earlier in the first century before Christ, belongs the first Greek novel of which we have certain record, and the first of which any part now remains. It set out the romantic story of Ninus, the founder of Nineveh, and a woman who, though not named in the surviving fragments, was presumably Semiramis. Although we possess only two small scraps of this, found on Egyptian papyri and first published in 1893, there is enough to show that it was an example, and perhaps not a very good example, of the class of ancient novels from which I have chosen the titular subject of this lecture. But it differed from them, possibly (though this cannot be

---

[1] *Appendix on the Greek Novel*, in the Loeb edition of *Daphnis and Chloe* and Parthenius, p. 410.

proved from such scanty evidence) in subordinating love to adventure, and certainly in purporting to relate the experiences of historical personages. In this latter respect it points back to such fictional treatment of history as we have found in Xenophon's *Cyropaedia*, and forward to such writings as the Alexander romance of the pseudo-Callisthenes, the earliest existing version of which has been dated at about 300 after Christ. Of the Alexander romance, although it falls outside the scope of our present study, it is relevant to observe that some of its components have been traced back to a time not long after the death of Alexander,[1] further proof that a form of historical fiction, at any rate, existed before the development of the Novel to which the *Ninus* fragments bear witness.

Another form of Greek prose fiction which calls for mention here is the wonder-tale, the tale of things marvellous, not to say incredible, experienced by travellers over distant lands and seas. This is the sort of tale that Lucian, in the second century, parodied so amusingly in his *Veracious History*, a work which is the prototype of *Baron Munchausen* and among the forbears of *Gulliver's Travels*. The German scholar Erwin Rohde, whose erudite work *Der griechische Roman und seine Vorläufer*, the first edition of which appeared as long ago as 1876, is still the fullest and best treatment of the Greek novel and its predecessors, thought that the Greek novel had its origin in the 'quite mechanical' combination of such wonder-tales with a love-story, the combination that is seen unmistakably in the tale of *The Incredible Things beyond Thule*, written by Antonius Diogenes in the

---

[1] See R. M. Rattenbury, in J. U. Powell's *New Chapters in the History of Greek Literature*, Third Series (Oxford, 1933), pp. 220 ff.

second century after Christ, of which we possess an
epitome made by the Byzantine Patriarch Photius.
But although in all the extant Greek novels there is a
love-story, and in all of them, except the *Daphnis and
Chloe*, an element of travel as well as of adventure, the
travels are over known lands and seas, and the adventures are at least not intended to surpass the bounds of
the credible, however severely they may tax our capa-
city for belief. For these and other reasons Rohde's
thesis must be regarded as unproven. The problem of
the origins of the Greek novel is complex, and for lack
of material it is not likely that a certain solution will
ever be attained. For our present purpose I shall be
content to draw attention to the sources, or at any rate
to some affinities, of particular features of the novels
which I have chosen for review.

All the extant Greek novels, if we leave out of account
the late Byzantine imitations, belong, as now seems
probable, to the second and third centuries after Christ,
though the fragments of the Ninus romance prove that
the novel, as a literary form, existed already in the first
century before Christ. I have said 'as now seems probable', because recent discovery has shown that views
long current as to the chronology of the novels must be
revised. Achilles Tatius, regarded with great likelihood
as the latest of the novelists, was thought by many
scholars, for instance by Rohde, to have lived in the
fifth century or even later; but the discovery by Grenfell
and Hunt of a part of the *Leucippe and Clitophon* in one of
the Oxyrhynchus papyri, the date of which can be fixed
on palaeographical evidence at little later than A.D.
300, brings him back into the third century or, at the
very latest, the beginning of the fourth. Similarly a

papyrus fragment of Chariton, who is accepted as the earliest of all, fixes his date at not later than 150 after Christ. It follows that between the first and the last of the extant novelists there is an interval, probably, of scarcely more than a century and a half. Other recently discovered papyri, fairly numerous though regrettably small and fragmentary, preserve scraps of novels, of which most seem to have been essentially of the same type as the extant novels, and all, excepting the Ninus romance, of the same period.[1]

The names of the Greek novels and their authors, in what may be accepted provisionally as their chronological order, are:

(1) *Chaereas and Callirrhoe*, by Chariton of Aphrodisias in Caria;
(2) *Habrocomes and Anthea*, otherwise called the *Ephesiaca*, by Xenophon of Ephesus;
(3) *Theagenes and Chariclea*, better known as the *Aethiopica*, by Heliodorus of Emesa in Syria;
(4) *Daphnis and Chloe*, by Longus;
(5) *Leucippe and Clitophon*, by Achilles Tatius of Alexandria.

Of two more novels of the same period we have only short abstracts made by the Byzantine Photius. These are:

(1) *The Incredible Things beyond Thule*, by Antonius Diogenes, to which I have already referred; and
(2) *The Babyloniaca*, by the Syrian Iamblichus, a tale of the ordinary love-and-adventure kind.

Also to be mentioned here is yet another tale of love and adventure, namely *Apollonius of Tyre*, by an

[1] For an excellent connected account of the light thrown on the Greek romances by recent papyrological discovery, I refer again to Rattenbury's chapter on Romance in Powell's *New Chapters*, Third Series.

unknown author, which, though it survives only in a Latin form, is thought, for reasons which seem to me to be valid, to be derived from a Greek original of the second century. Comparison with the other novels of the same class inclines me to think that it may be an abridged paraphrase of the Greek rather than a complete translation. *Apollonius of Tyre* is not distinguished by any peculiar excellence from other romances of its kind; but, having been turned into Latin early in the Middle Ages, it attained in Western lands a vogue that was denied to the rest, and that indeed was out of all proportion to its merit, and so exerted a remarkable influence in several of the literatures of Europe, including our own, through the course of many centuries. I mention, as one late but notable example, Shakespeare's use of this romance in his *Pericles Prince of Tyre*.

Of the authors of the Greek novels little is definitely known, and not much more can be conjectured. We do know, however, that most of them, if not all, were natives of Asia Minor or Syria or Egypt, countries of the 'Near East'; and this fact, together with the Eastern setting which they provide for many of their episodes, confirms in some measure the view, at which I have hinted more than once, that the Greek novel is, in part, the fruit of the contact of Hellas with the story-telling Orient.

As I have already remarked, the Greek novels are tales of love and travel and adventure, with the one exception of the *Daphnis and Chloe*, in which there is no travel at all and the element of adventure is not prominent. I have chosen the *Daphnis and Chloe* for treatment not only because it is unique in kind but also because, in my judgement, it is the best of the Greek novels.

My reasons for choosing the *Leucippe and Clitophon* are different, but not, I think, less adequate. Among the novels of the class to which it belongs, that of Chariton is of no extraordinary merit, and did not become known to the modern world, either in the original Greek or in translation, till the middle of the eighteenth century,[1] too late to have any direct influence on literature. Xenophon of Ephesus, first edited in 1726,[2] was also too late in the field, though one of his episodes seems to have made its way, by devious routes, into two of the Elizabethans; and his novel, though written with an admirable lucidity and grace of diction, is not in other respects to be ranked above any of the rest. There remain, in this group, Heliodorus and Achilles Tatius, two of the three—Longus is the third—who were translated into English during the reign of Elizabeth. Heliodorus, as the critics agree, is doubtless the better, though, as I think, his superiority consists less in positive merit than in the negative virtue of comparative freedom from the grosser forms of absurdity; he has also exerted a greater influence on later literature, though, as we shall see, the influence of Tatius is not negligible; nevertheless, I thought that, for the purpose of exemplification, that author should be preferred who, while in some respects inferior to the other, is more fully representative of the class, in defects as well as in merits: for there is no feature, good or bad, that is really characteristic of the Greek novel, but is exemplified in the *Leucippe and Clitophon*. I have also preferred

[1] First edition of the Greek, by D'Orville, 1750; first English translation, 1764.
[2] By Cocchia, London, 1726, with Latin translation. Salvini had published an Italian version, also at London, in 1723, three years before the *editio princeps* of the Greek. The first English translation was by Rooke, London, 1727.

the simplicity of Tatius to the extreme complexity of
Heliodorus, the author whom I read for pleasure to the
one whom I read from a sense of duty. My pleasure, it
is true, is not always of kinds that the reader was intended to experience.

The time has now come to present an ancient novelist
whose blood, I feel sure, ran in the veins of Mr. Edgar
Wallace, and who, were he alive to-day, would make a
fortune at Hollywood as a master of the 'feature-film'
scenario; of whom, nevertheless, one may say truly, in
the words of his Elizabethan translator, that 'there is
none who is learned, and desirous of good instructions,
which once having begun to read him, can lay him
aside, untill he have perused him over'.

Achilles Tatius, as we have seen, may be placed
with a high degree of probability in the third century
after Christ, and he is certainly not later than the beginning of the fourth century. Suidas the lexico-
grapher says that he was of Alexandria in Egypt, a
statement confirmed by some of the manuscripts of his
romance, by the praise of Alexandria in the fifth book,
and by the air of reality with which he invests some of
his Egyptian scenes. Suidas adds that he wrote, besides
the *Leucippe and Clitophon*, an account of many great and
wonderful men and some treatises on mathematical
and grammatical subjects; further, that he became a
Christian and a bishop. This last statement may be
safely rejected, and not only because there is no trace
of Christian feeling in Tatius' novel. Suidas would
seem to have transferred to Tatius, at least in part, the
famous story told about Heliodorus. It is related that
Heliodorus was Bishop of Tricca in Thessaly, and that
when required by his superiors either to resign his

bishopric or to destroy his *Aethiopica* he preferred to save the romance. Even this story is not true, but only well invented. Heliodorus the novelist was not a Christian, much less a bishop. But among the many bearers of the name Heliodorus there was, it seems, a Bishop of Tricca, and some ingenious person, having confused the two, composed an agreeable fiction which has remained current down to our own day.

The grammarian Thomas Magister, of the fourteenth century, says that Achilles Tatius was a 'rhetor' or orator, by which he doubtless means that he was a rhetorician and advocate, a 'sophist' of that 'new sophistic' which played so important a part in the intellectual life of the Graeco-Roman world in the first centuries of the Christian era and influenced so profoundly the literature of the period. Of these 'sophists' I shall have more to say later. Meanwhile let me observe that Thomas Magister's statement is confirmed by the internal evidence of style and episode. The only other references to Tatius in old writers—in Photius and Michael Psellos and in an epigram of the Palatine Anthology—consist in criticism of his work and tell us nothing about his life.

The *Leucippe and Clitophon* is preserved in a good many manuscripts, all of which, with the exception of the papyrus fragment to which I have referred, are of dates ranging from the thirteenth to the sixteenth century. The Greek text was first printed, at Heidelberg, in 1601, but its appearance was preceded by a number of sixteenth-century translations into Latin, Italian, French, and English, through which the novel became widely known among the educated. The first English translation, published in 1597, arrived too late for the makers of Elizabethan literature, who must therefore have used versions into other tongues, such as the Italian of Dolce or Coccio, the Latin of della Croce (otherwise 'Cruceius'), the French of Belleforest; but it has an independent value as a notable monument of Elizabethan prose. Its title-page bears the inscription: 'The| Most Delec=|table and pleasaunt Histo-|ry of *Clitophon* and *Leucippe*: | Written first in Greeke, by *Achilles Statius*, an | Alexandrian: and now newly transla-|*ted into English, By W. B.*' 'Statius', the name by which the author of the romance is here called, is a very old corruption of the true name Tatius. 'W. B.', the translator, was William Burton, the antiquarian, elder brother of the famous Robert Burton, author of the *Anatomy of Melancholy*, and he dedicated his version to Henry Wriothesley, third Earl of Southampton, the patron of Shakespeare. The fate of this version is remarkable. From 1597, the year of its publication, to 1897, exactly three centuries, no mention of it has been found anywhere. In 1897 a single copy was found, and this was acquired in 1916 by Mr. (now Sir) Stephen Gaselee. It was reprinted, with Introductions by Gaselee and Brett-Smith, in a limited edition published in 1923. While the sheets of this were being bound, another copy was discovered, and acquired by Gaselee in time to fill two small gaps in the earlier copy.

Burton, while mentioning on his title-page that the original of the romance is in Greek, does not claim, in so many words, to have made his translation from that tongue, though his readers might naturally have supposed that he had done so. Neither on his title-page, nor in the 'Epistle Dedicatorie', nor in the preface 'To the Curteous Reader', does he name his source; but the translation itself reveals that it was made, in the main, from the Latin of Cruceius. But only in the main; Gaselee's conjecture that Burton sometimes drew on another version I have been able to confirm by a clear example in the fourth book.[1]

The second English translation, long supposed to have been the first, was made by the Reverend Anthony Hodges, Rector of Wytham in Berks., and published anonymously at Oxford in 1638. Prefaced to it were laudatory poems contributed by eleven admirers of the translator, including, it seems, the translator ('A. H.') himself; among these is a poem, 'To the Ladies', by Richard Lovelace. Hodges makes no mention of Burton but may nevertheless have known his version. That he was deficient in candour may be reasonably inferred from the fact that he condemns Cruceius' translation, calling it, in Greek words quoted from Photius, 'loathly and abhorrent', but nevertheless used it in the making of his own version.[2]

And now, after so long a preamble, I come at last to the *Leucippe and Clitophon* itself. It may be read conveniently in the Loeb edition, in which the Greek text and Gaselee's version are given on opposite pages; less conveniently, perhaps, but with a pleasure not seriously diminished by the extreme inaccuracy of the translation, in the Elizabethan English of Burton. There is

---

[1] In iv. 3 the hippopotamus is trapped in a ξύλινον οἴκημα, a 'wooden cage', which Cruceius correctly translates *arca lignea*. But Burton's text gives 'a little coale made of boords', where, as Mr. R. G. Howarth has pointed out to me, 'coale' is a misprint for 'coate', i.e. 'cote'. Evidently, then, Burton used some translator who gave to οἴκημα, regardless of the context, its commoner meaning 'house' or 'dwelling'.

[2] I refer especially to the passage (iv. 3) quoted in the last footnote, where Hodges (p. 97) translates οἴκημα 'chest', an obvious misunderstanding of Cruceius' *arca lignea*.

also, in Bohn's Library, a translation by Rowland Smith.

The novel is in eight books, and bears the title *Erotica*, or *The Story of Leucippe and Clitophon*. The author tells us that while he was looking at a picture of Europa in the temple of Astarte at Sidon he fell into conversation with a young man named Clitophon who, standing by him, announced himself as one who had suffered much for love. The two men then retire to a plane-grove, where Clitophon relates the story of his love and adventures, which occupies the rest of the work. No attempt is made to give verisimilitude to this, either by making the author interrupt the narrative with question or comment or by reintroducing him at the end to round off the whole.

Clitophon was living with his father Hippias at Tyre and was about to marry, by his father's command, his half-sister Calligone. At this juncture Sostratus of Byzantium, the half-brother of Hippias, sends his wife Panthea and daughter Leucippe to Hippias at Tyre for refuge from the perils of a war. Clitophon, though affianced to Calligone, falls in love with his charming cousin Leucippe, but sees no hope of escaping the match that has been arranged for him. A dissolute young Byzantine named Callisthenes came to the rescue. Having heard of the beauty of Leucippe and fallen in love, by hearsay, with a girl whom he had never seen, he resolved to abduct her. Contriving to obtain appointment to a mission sent from Byzantium to Tyre, he got together a band of piratical ruffians and lay in wait for his prize on the occasion of a public sacrifice. But Leucippe, pretending illness, stayed at home; and Calligone, being seen with Panthea, whom

Callisthenes knew by sight, was seized by the gang and carried off to sea.

While feeling a proper regret for Calligone's misfortune, Clitophon 'breathed again'[1], as he says, at the unexpected cancellation of his wedding, and proceeded still more ardently with his wooing of Leucippe. Having persuaded her to receive him, he visits her in her chamber, but has no sooner been admitted than the girl's mother, Panthea, comes rushing in, having been disturbed by a dream in which a murderous assault was made upon her daughter. Clitophon makes his escape undetected, leaving Leucippe to face the angry mother. Leucippe, with a ready mendacity which, truth to tell, all the heroines of these ancient romances have at their command, and with an air of affronted virtue that is hardly warranted by the facts, sends her mother away baffled, if not convinced.

The lovers now decide to flee. Accompanied by the unscrupulous but faithful servant Satyrus, and by Clinias the cousin of Clitophon, they drive in a carriage to Berytus, the modern Beirout, whence they take ship for Alexandria. On board this ship they make the acquaintance of an Egyptian named Menelaus, a bereaved lover, the recital of whose sorrows leads to a debate on the theme of love. Here ends the second book.

On the third day of the voyage a great storm, which is described with obvious relish, wrecked the ship. Clitophon, floating with Leucippe on a piece of wreckage, prays to Poseidon, god of the sea, that, if they must die, they may be overwhelmed by the same wave or find a common tomb in the belly of the same fish.

---

[1] ἐγὼ δὲ ἀνέπνευσα.

However, the two come ashore safely at Pelusium in Egypt, and after a short rest hire a boat and proceed by the Nile towards Alexandria. On this voyage they were captured by brigands, who were presently attacked by an Egyptian force under Charmides. Clitophon escaped to Charmides, but left Leucippe a prisoner. The next day, looking across a deep fosse, he saw two men bring Leucippe to an altar, strap her down, and eviscerate her with a dagger. The entrails were then roasted on the altar, divided into small portions, and eaten by the brigands. The body was placed in a coffin, which was left on the spot when the brigands withdrew. At night Clitophon came out to end his life over his beloved's coffin; but when, after delivering a highly rhetorical address to the dead which is too ludicrous to be really revolting, he was about to stab himself, he saw, in the moonlight, two men running towards him. These proved to be Menelaus and Satyrus, who, having been saved from the shipwreck, had been captured by the brigands but allowed to join their company. Menelaus now opened the coffin, and out came Leucippe: not a pretty sight, poor lass, but alive and well. Menelaus and Satyrus, being entrusted with the task of sacrificing the maiden, had fitted her with a false abdomen made of thin sheepskin and filled with an animal's entrails and blood, and had used a theatrical dagger, the blade of which, excepting the tip, would retreat into the handle when any force was applied.

The three men, with the rescued Leucippe, find shelter with Charmides, the Egyptian general. Clitophon now begs Leucippe to crown his love, while they are 'in Fortune's calm' and before some even greater mischance befall them. But the goddess Artemis, in a dream, has bidden Leucippe remain virgin until she herself shall make her a bride, promising, however, that none other than Clitophon shall marry her. Clitophon, as he now remembers, has also been admonished in a dream, by Aphrodite, that he must wait for the completion of his happiness. Then Charmides falls in love with Leucippe, and is with difficulty repulsed. Gorgias, an Egyptian soldier, also falls in love with her, and tries to win her by administering a philtre; but as the servant who was charged with the task forgot to add water, the potion produced, not love, but a persistent and unseemly madness. After ten days, in the course of which Charmides went out to war and Gorgias was killed, a young man named Chaereas told the story of Gorgias' misdeed and furnished an antidote to the philtre. Leucippe recovers, and an overjoyed but tactless Clitophon tells her of her madness.

We have now reached the fifth book. As the Nile is now clear of bandits, hero and heroine, with Menelaus and Satyrus and Chaereas, sail for Alexandria, which they reach in three days. Chaereas, enamoured of Leucippe, invites them to his birthday party at Pharos, the island on which stood the famous lighthouse. As they were setting out, a hawk chasing a swallow struck Leucippe with his wing; and Clitophon saw, in a painter's studio, a picture of the rape of Philomel. Perturbed by these omens, they turn back. The next day Chaereas comes with a renewal of his invitation, which they cannot with any show of decency refuse. Menelaus pleads an indisposition and stays behind, but Clitophon and Leucippe accompany their host in a boat to Pharos. In the evening a band of pirates, hired by Chaereas, rush in, wound Clitophon in the thigh,

and carry Leucippe off to their ship. The commander
of the island garrison goes in pursuit, taking Clitophon
on board in a litter. But the pirates, finding themselves
pursued, bring the girl up on deck, cut off her head, and
fling her body into the sea. The body is retrieved, and
the pursuers, finding that the pirates have now been
reinforced by a second ship, turn back. Clitophon
gives the body burial after kissing the severed neck and
lamenting, in elaborate rhetoric, that his beloved is
divided between land and sea, and that the sea, though
it has the smaller part, has that part, the head, which is
really all.

Clitophon now returns to Alexandria, where he encounters Clinias, whom he had supposed to have been
lost in the shipwreck. Clinias had been picked up and
taken to Sidon, whence he had made his way home to
Tyre. There he learnt that, on the day after the flight
of the lovers, a letter had come from Sostratus betroth-
ing Leucippe to Clitophon, so that the flight had been
unnecessary, no more than a cruel stroke of Fortune.
Hearing afterwards from a voyager that Clitophon had
been seen in Egypt, he had arrived eight days before to
search for him.

Satyrus, supported by Clinias, now urges him to
marry Melitte, a very rich and beautiful young widow
from Ephesus, who has fallen in love with him. Leucippe is dead, and Melitte offers him ease and luxury
and love. Clitophon, though unwillingly, consents, and
acknowledges, when he has met the lady, that she is not
unattractive and that he received her kiss not without
pleasure. He stipulates, however, that the marriage
shall be marriage only in name until they reach Ephesus, since he has made a vow to abstain from love till he

is gone from the regions in which Leucippe died. The marriage takes place, but both at Alexandria and on the voyage to Ephesus Clitophon resists, by pleading his vow, the importunities of poor love-sick Melitte.

Arrived at Ephesus, they proceed to Melitte's estate a short distance from the city. In the garden a slave-woman, scantily clad and in fetters, throws herself at Melitte's feet and begs protection from the steward Sosthenes who had bought her from pirates and would offer her violence. She gives her name as Lacaena, her country as Thessaly. At dinner that evening Satyrus arrives with a letter for Clitophon—from Leucippe; for the ill-used slave-girl, of course, was she. Not in anger, but in love and sorrow, she reminds Clitophon of all that she has endured for his sake, keeping herself unsullied still to be his bride, while he has now married another woman. She begs him to show his gratitude by going bail for her purchase-money and sending her home. Clitophon, in his reply, assures her that, in spite of appearances, he too has been faithful, and promises to make his defence soon.

Finding that Leucippe is alive, Clitophon cannot, as he says, even look at another woman, but of course he does not dare to tell Melitte that Lacaena is Leucippe. He makes excuses, which Melitte does not believe but cannot choose but accept. Melitte, supposing that Leucippe is a Thessalian and therefore skilled in all magic arts, asks her—note the irony of the situation—to prepare a love-philtre so that the coldness of Clitophon may be overcome. This incident is ingeniously contrived, for Leucippe learns thus that her lover has in fact been true. The same day, while Clitophon was taking wine with Melitte and trying to invent new means of evasion, there was a sudden uproar, and Thersander, the chief villain of the piece, rushed into the house. Thersander was the husband of Melitte, supposed to have been drowned at sea some months before. Ignoring Melitte's open arms, he gives our most unheroic hero a severe thrashing, at the end of which Clitophon inquires mildly 'Who are you, sir? Why have you assailed me thus?' Thersander, after further violence, has him put into chains and locked up in an outhouse. While he was being beaten, Clitophon had dropped Leucippe's letter, and Melitte, finding it, understands all. Thersander, having worked off his rage, goes to the house of a friend. Melitte, visiting Clitophon in his prison, upbraids him bitterly, but passing from invective to love and pleading wins from him the consolation of one loving embrace. She then sets him free, giving him money and disguising him in her own clothes. Soon, however, he was caught by Thersander and Sosthenes and clapped into jail on a charge of adultery.

Meanwhile Thersander makes persistent and violent love to Leucippe, of whom he had been told by Sosthenes, visiting her in the country whither she had gone to collect herbs for Melitte's philtre. Foiled by her inexpugnable virtue, he determines to get rid of Clitophon. At the beginning of the seventh book he incites the jailer to poison his prisoner. The jailer is afraid to do this, but consents to introduce into Clitophon's cell, in the guise of an arrested criminal, a man who, by Thersander's instructions, tells with circumstantial detail how he has killed Leucippe as the hired assassin of Melitte. Clitophon, believing this story, wishes to die, and resolves to confess that he plotted with Melitte for the commission of the murder.

In the last two books we read, at somewhat wearisome length, of the trial of Clitophon; of his confession; of the speeches of prosecutor and accused and advocates; of another thrashing which Clitophon, unresisting, receives from Thersander; of how Leucippe, having escaped, takes refuge in the temple of Artemis[1] but is accused by Thersander of being both slave and harlot. Sostratus, the father of Leucippe, arrives during the trial and gives to Clitophon, as the self-confessed murderer of his daughter, yet another beating, but of course is reconciled when the daughter is found to be alive. Leucippe, submitting voluntarily to a trial of chastity in the grotto of Artemis, is proved pure by the sweet music of the pipes of Pan. In the end all is well: Thersander, discomfited, takes to flight, the lovers are united. Clitophon relates his adventures during their separation, omitting, in order to spare Leucippe's feelings and to save his own face, the particulars of his parting from Melitte. Leucippe, in turn, explains her own reappearance. The pirates, wishing to stop the pursuit, had dressed in Leucippe's clothes a woman whom they had on board, cut off her head, and cast the body into the sea. Her abductor Chaereas, who alone had wished to do her violence, was murdered by one of the pirates. Sostratus gives news of Calligone. The dissolute young Callisthenes, after carrying her off in mistake for Leucippe, had respected her maidenhood, conceived an honourable love for her, and, under the influence of this love, repented of his evil ways. Having by this time proved himself admirable in peace

[1] i.e. of 'Diana of the Ephesians'.

and war, he was now suing to Hippias for her hand in marriage.

All now sail from Ephesus to Byzantium, where Leucippe and Clitophon are married. Passing thence to Tyre, they arrive just in time for the wedding of Calligone and Callisthenes.

Here the story ends. But the author, being a professional rhetorician, has not been content with the telling of a simple, if sensational, tale. He must embellish the narrative with the artifices that are proper to his trade, and must instruct and edify his readers by interlarding it with extracts from a copious book of commonplaces. Most of these extraneous ornaments, however, though but loosely attached to the story, are very well devised and executed; and if, as sometimes happens, they have little or no relevance to the plot, they do not cause any such intolerable suspension of interest as occurs repeatedly, for instance, in the *Aethiopica* of Heliodorus. They are of various kinds. There are elaborate descriptions of paintings: Europa and the Bull; Andromeda and Perseus; the torture and rescue of Prometheus; the rape of Philomel. In respect of subject, two, and only two, of these are relevant: the representation of Europa moves Clitophon to the recital of his own experience of Love, while the rape of Philomel is an omen of the impending abduction of Leucippe by the pirates; and the descriptions of all four, though excellent in themselves, are mere purple patches designed to display the rhetorician's skill in translating painted pictures into words.

Rudyard Kipling will tell you how the elephant got his trunk: Achilles Tatius will tell you how he got his breath. Let me read from Burton's translation. The Egyptian Charmides once saw a Greek put his head into the mouth of an elephant so that the monster's sweet breath might cure his headache.[1] Now Burton:

'Then said I, how commeth it to passe that so deformed a creature hath so sweete a savour? Of his meate (said *Charmides*) whereof hee feedeth: the countrey of the *Indians* is very neere the sunne, and they be the first people which inhabite the East, and do feele the force of his beames more hot. In *Greece* there groweth a flower, which in *India* is not a flower but a blossom, such as those which grow upon trees: as it groweth it hath no savour, neither is in any estimation, whether because it will give no pleasure where it is knowen, or whether it do envie his countreymen: but if it be carried a little out of his countrey, it yeeldeth a sweete and odoriferous savour, that is the *Indian* flower which is commonly called the blacke rose: uppon this Elephants do feede in those countries, as Oxen do of grasse amongst us, wherfore beeing fed with so sweet meat, they cannot choose but send forth a sweete breath.'

The elephant, you observe, gets his breath from eating cloves.

Tatius teems with as many 'cheerful facts' as Gilbert's Major-General. His description of the crocodile, at the end of the fourth book, is as good as you will find anywhere, even in Herodotus; and he is no less 'informative' on such diverse topics as the hippopotamus and the phœnix and the discovery of purple. On love, of course, he is a high authority: love, even, among birds and beasts and snakes and plants and metals: is it not love that attracts the iron to the magnet,

---

[1] iv. 4–5. The Elder Pliny, xxviii. 24 (8), says that the touch of an elephant's trunk cures headache, 'more effectively if the beast also sneezes'.

is not their touch a kind of kiss? You will also encounter, among the ornaments of the romance, an excellent
example of the Oriental beast-fable:[1] how the tiny but
presumptuous and arrogant gnat, having taunted the
great lion into a fury, escaped his savage jaws only to
be caught ignominiously in a spider's web.

As in these incidentals, so also in the body of the
narrative the arts and practice of the sophist-rhetorician are made manifest. It is easy to mock at them,
and the kindliest critic must confess that they sometimes issue in exquisite absurdity. Is there a storm at
sea?[2] Our author, perfect pattern of a land-lubber,
describes it in detail: how, as the gale blew now from
this quarter now from that, and the ship rolled scuppers-
under, the passengers dashed from side to side in the
endeavour to trim ship, and thus ran 'a sort of long-
distance race' (λόλιχόν τινα λρόμον) all day, carrying
their baggage in their hands; how when the crew, led
by the skipper, had jumped into the lifeboat, a strong
young man, grabbing the painter, pulled it alongside
again; and so forth, till our friends, on their respective
pieces of wreckage, shout to one another over the
raging sea. Even more ludicrous is Clitophon's apo-
strophe to Leucippe[3] after she has been sacrificed, as he
supposes, by the brigands. Here is a small part of it:

'. . . They divided up the mysteries of thy belly, and
accursed were the altar and the coffin that brought thee
sepulture. Thy body lies here: but thy bowels where? If
the fire had consumed them, less grievous had been thy
fate; but now the sepulture of thy bowels has become the
sustenance of bandits.'

In these episodes you have the rhetorician at his

[1] ii. 21–2.   [2] iii. 1–5.   [3] iii. 16.

worst. More often his art appears in a mere sophistication of style, a Euphuism, that is not without charm.
Apart from his occasional extravagances, Achilles
Tatius is one of the most pleasant of the late writers,
master of a Greek which, if not classical, is at any rate
comparable in respect of smoothness and clarity with
the best work of the great age.

Chariton, author of the *Chaereas and Callirrhoe*, writes
at the beginning of his eighth book: 'In this Book you
shall find not brigandage and slavery and trial-at-law,
fighting and heroism, war and capture, but honourable loves and lawful wedlock.' There you have the
chief constituents, not only of *Chaereas and Callirrhoe*, but
also of *Leucippe and Clitophon* and of all the romances of
their class: a pair of lovers, separation and suffering,
the conflict of virtue with villainy, virtue triumphant,
reunion and happiness at the end. They are still serving
their turn at the present day. And yet out of these
constant and simple ingredients, variously combined
and variously spiced, such diversity of dishes has been
prepared that each has a savour and an interest of
its own.

In one aspect, as has been said, the *Leucippe and
Clitophon* is a panegyric of chastity; and the same is
true, in greater or less degree, of most of the Greek
novels. The exaltation of this virtue, as a dominant
motive, is something new in Western literature. The
heroine successfully resists both temptation and violence, the hero remains no less constant to his one love.
Of lapses I can recall only three. In Chariton the
heroine Callirrhoe, finding herself pregnant by her lost
husband, consents, in the interest of the child, to marry
another man who will think himself the father. In

Achilles Tatius both hero and heroine offend. For although, before the flight, the assignation of the two did not achieve its object, it was assignation none the less; and while Clitophon, when he married Melitte, had the excuse of believing that Leucippe was dead, he had not that excuse, though he had others, for his parting embrace.

Of these defects in his plot and in his drawing of hero and heroine Tatius was presumably unconscious. Like his fellow novelists, he is not strong in psychology; and, like them, he allows the course of the story to be determined, in great part, not by the development and interplay of characters but by the operation of external and superhuman forces, of which the chief is Fortune, a wanton and uncontrollable Chance. So episode follows episode, and adventure adventure, until Fortune or some other Power brings the desired end. When Fortune had caused the abduction of Calligone, we are to understand that she was given up as lost, so that there was no longer any reason why Clitophon should not marry Leucippe. Yet they continue to practise concealment. Leucippe's father wrote from Byzantium giving his consent to the marriage, and only Fortune determined that the letter should arrive the day after their totally unnecessary flight. When the lovers, saved from the shipwreck, landed in Egypt, it was not obdurate virtue but the admonition of Artemis, given in a dream, that kept Leucippe from Clitophon's arms. Clitophon's love for Leucippe is real, but first Aphrodite and then Fortune determine that, except for the payment of one debt of charity, he shall match his sweetheart's fidelity.

In character-drawing Tatius does not excel. In his

beautiful and virtuous young heroine there is little that is individual, little to distinguish her from the other heroines of the Greek novels. She might even seem colourless and insipid, were it not for her splendid denunciation of the lustful Thersander[1] and for the love and gentleness that inform her letter of reproach and appeal to Clitophon.[2] Clitophon, alas, is a spiritless fellow who has better luck than he deserves. For all his devotion, he is moved more by his own sufferings than by those of the girl; he sophisticates with his conscience; when he is thrashed, as happens thrice, he does not resist: he can do no better than express gratification because the assailant has cut a hand on his teeth.[3] Thersander, the husband whose return rescues Clitophon from his awkward predicament, is much better conceived: no Enoch Arden, but a violent and vicious brute whom any widow might have been glad to forget in a second marriage, and whose vices increase our sympathy with Melitte and go far towards justifying her subsequent appeal for one token of Clitophon's love. Melitte is best of all, the one complete success in character-drawing that Tatius has achieved: a young and charming woman, deeply in love; sorely ill-used by her new husband, yet preserving a sense of humour which enables her to jest about her misfortune; loving to the end, but helping Clitophon to escape and rejoin his sweetheart when she realizes that her own union with him cannot endure; with too much of the sensual, perhaps, in her love, yet winning and retaining our esteem.

'Who ever loved', asks the poet, 'that loved not at first sight?' Love at first sight is among the constants

[1] vi. 20 ff.   [2] v. 18.   [3] viii. 1.

of the Greek romances: the two young people meet, or at least see one another, and the deed is done. Thus, in Xenophon of Ephesus, Habrocomes, aged sixteen, too conscious of his beauty and scornful of Love, sees Anthea, aged fourteen, in her best frock among the maidens at a festival of Artemis, and at once falls a victim to the god whom he had contemned. Anthea, on her part, is immediately enthralled by Habrocomes' beauty, and so far disregards what 'becomes a young woman'[1] as to speak loudly, so that Habrocomes may overhear her, and to reveal as much as possible[2] of her person. Achilles Tatius does not fall into any such absurdity, but, regardless of precedent and with greater truth to life, describes a wooing and the ripening of love. This is managed with considerable skill and, at times, very charmingly. One incident will serve as illustration.[3] Clitophon had seen Leucippe cure a bee-sting on her maid's hand by murmuring an Egyptian charm over it. A little later, he pretends to have been stung on the lip, and begs her to repeat the charm:

'Putting my hand to my face, I pretended to have been stung and to be in pain. She came to me and pulled away my hand and asked me where I had been hurt. And I said, "On the lip. But won't you say the charm, dear?" So she came and put her mouth on the place to say the charm, and whispered something while gently brushing my lips. And I kept kissing her stealthily and silently, while she, opening and closing her lips as she whispered the charm, turned the charm to kisses. Then at last, flinging my arms round her, I kissed her openly. Releasing herself, she cried: "What are you doing? Are you saying a charm also?" "I am kissing

---

[1] τῶν παρθένοις πρεπόντων, a happy anticipation of Mrs. Malaprop's phrase.
[2] μέρη τοῦ σώματος . . . τὰ δυνατά.   [3] ii. 7.

the enchantress", I answered, "for your curing of my pain."
As she understood me and smiled, I took heart and said:
"Ah, my dear, I have been wounded again, more grievously:
for the wound has sped down to my heart and needs your
charm. Surely you too must have a bee on your lips, for you
are full of honey, and your kisses wound." '

Sophisticated, if you like; but what could be more
prettily done?

Of some of the elements that are common to these
novels—the dreams and omens, for instance, and the
pirates and brigands—I defer consideration to the next
lecture. Others I have already touched upon, others
call for mention here. In both Chariton and Achilles
Tatius the hero is brought to trial and voluntarily confesses himself the murderer of his beloved whom he
falsely believes to be dead. The rhetorician, moving,
as he too often does, in a world of vain imaginings, is
not deterred by the flagrant improbability of this, but
is resolved on the one hand to demonstrate the potency
of Love, who can make a man prefer the most shameful
of deaths to his survival of the loved one, and on the
other hand to find an opportunity of displaying his own
mastery of the pleader's arts. If, in thus killing two
birds with one stone, Tatius borrows unashamedly
from Chariton, what matter? That sense of literary
ownership by which we set such store is of modern
growth. Chariton, to mention only one other instance,
has his hero Chaereas rescued when on the point of
crucifixion; Xenophon of Ephesus, writing perhaps in
the same generation, does not scruple to transfer the
adventure to his Habrocomes. They all did it, and no
one thought any the worse of them.

Of hairbreadth escapes, too, and of the apparent

death of the heroine, you will find plenty of examples, though not many, perhaps, are quite so startling as those which enliven the *Leucippe and Clitophon*. Tatius, magnificently bold, makes his hero see Leucippe first disembowelled and then beheaded. In Heliodorus a blow is struck in the dark and kills, not the heroine, for whom it was intended, but another woman who deserved to die. In Chariton and Xenophon the heroine appears to die, is placed in a tomb, regains her senses there, and is found by robbers who come to rifle the tomb. But note an important difference. In Chariton[1] the hero, persuaded by some miscreants that his young wife is admitting a lover, kicks her 'with good aim' (εὐστόχως), as we are told, but still regrettably, in the diaphragm, and leaves her for dead. In Xenophon[2] of Ephesus the heroine, in her despair, bribes a physician to brew her a poisonous philtre, but receives from him a sleeping-draught that produces only the semblance of death. The philtre, in its various forms, plays a notable part in the ancient romances. It appears twice, as we have seen, in *Leucippe and Clitophon*, and you will meet it again in Book X of the *Golden Ass*, where, as here, a doctor substitutes a sleeping-draught for the desired poison. But the episode in Xenophon of Ephesus is of peculiar interest in that it is an anticipation, and perhaps the ultimate source, of the philtre incident in Shakespeare's *Romeo and Juliet*.[3] Chambers,[4] who is among those who hold this opinion, strangely overlooks the still more striking resemblance of the incident in *Cymbeline*[5] where the Queen, wishing to kill Imogen, receives from the physician not poison but a narcotic.

[1] i. 4, at end.   [2] iii. 5 ff.   [3] iv. 1.
[4] E. K. Chambers, *William Shakespeare*, vol. i, pp. 346 and 487.   [5] i. 5.

Why conjecture that this may be derived from the
Golden Ass, if the other, through however long a line,
descends from Xenophon of Ephesus? A similar device
is used in Dekker's *Satiro-mastix*, where, as in Xenophon,
the motive for taking poison is the avoidance of dis-
honour. In all these stories, ancient and modern, of
philtres (or kicks) that produce the appearance of
death, it is irrelevant to observe that the thing is impossible, that the evidences of death are unmistakable,
for we are not to judge the world of the imagination by
the world of humdrum reality; but Shakespeare, I suppose, is the only writer who takes the bull by the horns,
so to speak, and invites the matter-of-fact critic to do
his worst, when, in *Romeo and Juliet*, he makes Capulet
proclaim the fulfilment of Friar Lawrence's promise:

> Out, alas! she's cold;
> Her blood is settled, and her joints are stiff;
> Life and these lips have long been separated:
> Death lies on her like an untimely frost
> Upon the sweetest flower of all the field.

But I have been digressing. Achilles Tatius is distinguished, among the Greek novelists, by the element
of humour which occasionally brightens his narrative.
There is joking at the expense of the sly and curmud-
geonly slave Conops, the perfect exemplar of a spoil-
sport; there is Melitte's pathetic jest at her own expense,
when she says that she has had a unique experience:
others have seen a ceno*taph*, but only she a ceno*gam*—
an empty marriage, a marriage without a husband;
there is Thersander's caustic humour[1] when Leucippe
protests her respectability: 'Were the pirates a pack of
philosophers? Did none of them have eyes?' and there

[1] vi. 21 φιλοσόφων ἦν τὸ πειρατήριον; οὐδεὶς ἐν αὐτοῖς εἶχεν ὀφθαλμούς;

is humour, of a less pleasant kind, in the taunting of Thersander by the priest of Artemis at Ephesus, who possesses, and displays, a most unpriestly acquaintance with Aristophanes.

As in the other novels, so also in the *Leucippe and Clitophon* there is some dialogue, but no real conversation. Except in the forms which it assumes in drama, conversation, of which the modern novel makes such great and effective use, had not yet been translated into literature.

It will be remembered that at the end of the tale we are told how Calligone, Clitophon's half-sister and affianced bride, had fared after her abduction by Callisthenes. This story, though merely sketched and appended to the main narrative, is of great historical interest. It indicates the possibility of a romance of a kind which ancient literature, so far as our records show, was never to produce, but of which the literature of later times and other peoples was to exhibit many notable examples, introducing, for the first time, the element of chivalry[1] into the love of man for maid, and employing, also for the first time, as dominant idea, the refining and ennobling influence of a good woman. In this, if in nothing else, Achilles Tatius makes good his claim to immortality.

It has become evident, I hope, that the *Leucippe and Clitophon*, though marred by many blemishes and falling far short of greatness, is nevertheless not altogether contemptible. But apart from any merit inherent in his work, Tatius has this secondary title to fame, that he is among those authors of the Greek romances who have brought something to the making of modern

[1] Wolff, *Greek Romances in Elizabethan Fiction*, p. 132.

literature. As we have seen, he became known in the sixteenth century, before the first printing of the Greek text, through translations into various languages; and Tasso, already, in his pastoral *Aminta*, imitates the charming episode of the bee and the kiss, an example followed, in the next century, by Honoré d'Urfé in his pastoral romance *Astrée*. One may mention, in passing, that the Birnam Wood incident in *Macbeth* has a fairly close parallel in an episode of the fourth book of *Leucippe and Clitophon*. The robbers, threatened with an assault, furnish the old men, in the front rank, with branches of palm-trees, so that, as the whole force advances, the fighting-men, trailing their spears, are concealed by the foliage. But Rohde gives good reasons for believing that Tatius was here using an old fable, of Eastern origin, which appears independently in a number of literatures, and that, in spite of the resemblance, he was not among those who transmitted the story to Shakespeare.

The real importance of Tatius, in this aspect, lies in his contributions to Elizabethan prose fiction and, through this, to the making of the modern novel. With Heliodorus, though in less measure, he furnished structure and material for Sidney's *Arcadia*, and thus was among the influences that formed the novels of Richardson and Walter Scott; of Greene, as Dr. S. L. Wolff[1] puts it, he was the 'first and latest love'; in Lyly himself, and not only in him, we recognize Tatius as one of the sources of English Euphuism.

[1] For a full discussion of these matters, the reader is referred to Dr. Wolff's thorough and valuable study, *Greek Romances in Elizabethan Fiction* (Columbia University Press, 1912).

II

'DAPHNIS AND CHLOE'

LIST OF CHIEF CHARACTERS

A'stylus: son of Dionysophanes
Chlo'e: a shepherdess
Chro'mis: a farmer
Cleari'sta: wife of Dionysophanes
Da'phnis: a goatherd
Dionyso'phanes: a citizen of Mytilene, father of Daphnis
Dor'kōn (Dorco): a young herdsman
Dry'as: a shepherd, foster-father to Chloe
Gna'thōn: parasite to Astylus

La'mōn: a goatherd, foster-father to Daphnis
Lam'pis: a rejected suitor of Chloe
Lykai'nion (Lycaenium): wife of Chromis
Me'gacles: a citizen of Mytilene
Myr'tale: wife of Lamon
Na'pe: wife of Dryas
Phile'tas: an old herdsman
Tyrian Pirates
Young Huntsmen from Methy'mna

T HE *Leucippe and Clitophon* of Achilles Tatius served us as a typical representative of those tales of love and travel and adventure which constitute the largest of the classes into which the Greek novels may be distributed. We now turn to the *Daphnis and Chloe*, an example, unique in ancient literature, of the pastoral romance. Its first English translator, Angell Daye (1587), thus announces it on his title-page: '*Daphnis and Chloe* | excellently | describing the weight | of affection, the simplicitie of love, the purport | of honest meaning, the resolution of men, and disposi-|tion of Fate, finished in a Pastorall'. And that his praise was sincere may be inferred from the fact that he 'interlaced' it 'with the praises | of a most peerlesse Princesse, wonderfull in Maiestie, | and rare in perfection, celebrated within | the same Pastorall'. The 'peerlesse Princesse' was Elizabeth, strangely imported into an ancient romance. Daye's next successor, George Thornley (1657), announces 'Daphnis and Chloe | a most sweet and pleasant pastoral romance for young ladies'.[1] Pleasant indeed is this romantic tale of goatherd and shepherdess; and sweet, too, with a sweetness somewhat cloying, perhaps, to modern taste; but that it is a 'romance for young ladies' not all will agree. We must take it as we find it. Unless my judgement is seriously at fault, there is at least no plying of that muck-rake which to-day is the favourite tool of so many novelists.

The full title of the romance may be paraphrased *The Lesbian Pastorals of Daphnis and Chloe*. Of its author Longus, one of a considerable number of writers who bore a Latin name but wrote in Greek, very little may be said to be known. Indeed, even his name has been in dispute, but only because some scholars whose ingenuity exceeded their common sense drew false inferences from a copyist's error. His date is matter of conjecture. He is not mentioned by any other writer before the Byzantine age, and himself mentions no historical name or event. His borrowings, so far as they can be identified, are from writers who lived centuries before any possible date that can be assigned to him; from Theocritus, for instance, who belongs to the earlier part of the third century before Christ. But considerations of language and comparison with the other novelists make it likely that he wrote about the middle of the third century after Christ, a little earlier, perhaps, than Achilles Tatius. His birthplace, of course, is unknown, but one may infer from the tale itself that he had some

---

[1] J. M. Edmonds, who in his edition of *Daphnis and Chloe* for the Loeb Library prints a revised Thornley opposite the Greek, accuses Thornley of allowing the 'young ladies' to suppose that the romance was his original work. But in the Epistle Dedicatory 'To Young Beauties' Thornley plainly distinguishes the Author from himself, and in the preface 'To the Criticall Reader' he names as author 'Longus Sophista'. Edmonds errs again in saying that Longus and Horace are 'the only literary users of the name Chloe': Martial has the name thrice.

association, whether by birth or merely by residence, with the island of Lesbos.

One of his earliest editors, Jungermann (1605), whose edition with Latin translation was used by Thornley, calls him 'Longus the Sophist'. Jungermann's authority for the title, if he had any, is no longer discoverable; but the romance itself reveals plainly that Longus, like the other Greek novelists, was in fact a 'sophist'. The name *sophistes* had been given as far back as Socrates' day to men who taught *sophia* for a fee: that is, to professional teachers of 'wisdom'. Early in the Christian era the name acquired a new significance and was assigned to rhetoricians who practised public declamation and earned a living partly as advocates in the courts and partly as public entertainers. A great part of the literature of the second and third centuries was a product of this 'New Sophistic'. The work of these sophist-rhetoricians can be recognized by unmistakable marks of their trade, among which are artificialities in vocabulary and in structure of sentence and paragraph; addiction to speech-making; a fondness for the episode; love of elaborate ornament whether in description or in speech; and so many of these characteristics appear in the *Daphnis and Chloe* that Longus' membership of the class cannot be doubted. But to call him a sophist is not to condemn him: we shall find that the *Daphnis and Chloe* is no mere curiosity of literature but a work of high merit.

Like the *Leucippe and Clitophon*, it begins with a picture. The author, hunting in Lesbos, saw in a grove of the Nymphs a beautiful painted picture and was moved to tell in words the story that it suggested.

'And therefore', he writes (I quote from Thornley's translation), 'when I had carefully sought, and found an Interpreter of the Image, I drew up these four Books; A Perpetuall Oblation to Love; an everlasting Anathema, Sacred to Pan and the Nymphs; and a Delightful Possession, even for all men. For this will cure him that is sick; and rouze him that is in dumps; one that has loved, it will remember of it; one that has not, it will instruct. For there was never any yet that wholly could escape Love, and never shall there be any: never, so long as beauty shall be; never, so long as eyes can see. But help me God[1] to write with wisdom and proportion, the Passions, and wonderfull fortunes of others; and while I write of their Loves, keep me in my own right Wits.'

After this preamble, he relates the story of which I now give a summary.

Once upon a time, on the estate of a rich man of Mytilene, the goatherd Lamon, looking for a lost she-goat, came into a thicket. Here he found the she-goat giving suck to a baby boy. Beside the boy were some precious 'recognition-tokens' (γνωρίσματα) of purple cloth and gold and ivory. Resisting the temptation to take the tokens and leave the baby, he took both home to his wife Myrtale, and they brought the boy up as their own child, giving to him the pastoral name Daphnis.

Two years later, the shepherd Dryas made a similar discovery. For in a grotto of the Nymphs he found a baby girl being suckled by a ewe, and with her also there were recognition-tokens of gold. He took the babe to his wife Nape, who mothered her and called her by the pastoral name Chloe.

When Daphnis was fifteen years old and Chloe thir-

----

[1] i.e. Eros, Love.

teen, the foster-parents, obeying dreams sent by the Nymphs, sent them out to tend goats and sheep in the same field. Thus the two children, goatherd and shepherdess, worked together and played together, and soon became fast friends. One day Daphnis fell into a deep pit that had been dug to catch a wolf that was preying on the flocks and herds, and was pulled out by Chloe with the help of the herdsman Dorkon. And so Chloe went with him to the grotto of the Nymphs and stood by while he washed the soil of the pit from him in the spring. Never before had he seemed so fair to her, and from her admiration of his beauty there arose within her a mysterious longing which, though she knew it not, was love. Meanwhile Dorkon the neatherd had fallen in love with Chloe. He and Daphnis engaged in a contest of self-praise, each endeavouring to prove himself the better and handsomer. (You note here the borrowing from the pastoral poets.) The prize for the victor was a kiss from Chloe. Daphnis won the day, and the touch of Chloe's lips sowed in him also the seeds of love, though he, like her, could not understand what troubled his spirit. Dorkon now became a professed suitor for Chloe's hand, making gifts to her foster-father Dryas, who, however, rejected him. Thereupon he resolved to seize her by force, and to accomplish his purpose disguised himself in a wolf-skin and lay in wait for her. But the sheep-dogs attacked him so fiercely that he was with difficulty rescued from them by Daphnis and Chloe. These forgave him, thinking that he had but played upon them a rustic jest.

Some time afterwards, the peaceful country-side was invaded by Tyrian pirates who carried off much booty

of wine and grain and honey and cattle to their ship.
And with their booty they took Daphnis, who called
loudly on the name of Chloe. Chloe ran in search of
Dorkon, whom she found sorely wounded by the
marauders and at the point of death. But before he
died he gave her his herdsman's pipes and bade her
play upon them the tune which he had taught to her
and Daphnis in happier days. Then, with Chloe's
farewell kiss as his reward, he died. But Chloe played
upon the pipes, and at the music the captured cattle
leapt helter-skelter from the pirate ship, overturning it
in the sea. And the pirates, weighed down by their
armour, were all drowned, but Daphnis, with the
cattle, swam ashore. He and Chloe gave to the body
of Dorkon fitting burial.

Summer was now past, and autumn came. Daphnis
and Chloe took part in the work and merrymaking of
the vintage. When this was over, they returned to their
goats and sheep. An old herdsman, Philetas, tells them
how one morning in his garden the winged god Eros,
Love, had appeared before him and revealed that he
had chosen Daphnis and Chloe to be his especial
favourites. And therewith Philetas told them something of the nature of that love which had long since
troubled and mystified them. While they were still
pondering the purport of what Philetas had told them,
the peace of their pastures was again disturbed. Some
wealthy young men from Methymna, sailing along the
coast, landed to enjoy a day's hunting. They moored
their vessel to the shore with an improvised rope of
plaited willow-twigs. But while they were absent at
the hunt, goats from Daphnis's herd wandered down
to the beach and ate the rope, so that the vessel went

adrift out to sea. Furious at this, the young men seized Daphnis, but the country-folk rallied to his aid and prevented them from carrying him off. The matter was submitted to Philetas as arbiter, and his verdict was in favour of Daphnis. The young men, returning home, reported that they had been assaulted and robbed. Thereupon the Methymnaeans sent an expedition of ten ships which ravaged the coast. Chloe was taken prisoner. Daphnis was in despair, but the Nymphs, in a dream, reassured him. The god Pan so terrified the Methymnaeans that they liberated Chloe and the captured herds. Chloe's return was celebrated by a rustic festival, and she and Daphnis swore to one another undying fidelity.

Winter comes, and the snow, lying deep over the country-side, confines all the folk to their huts. Daphnis finds time a laggard while he is parted from his sweetheart. He goes bird-catching among the myrtles by Dryas' house, but can find no excuse for entering. However, as he is about to return home, Dryas comes running out in pursuit of a dog that has stolen some meat, finds Daphnis there, and invites him in. Daphnis spends the night with his friends, and in the morning plights his troth anew to Chloe. At last spring returns, and the young lovers, now reunited, drive their herds out once more to pasture. With the spring stirring in their veins, youth and maiden busy themselves once more with thoughts of love, but still do not fully understand its meaning. Lykainion, the wife of a neighbour, supplements for Daphnis the lesson that Philetas had given, but he does not impart his new knowledge to Chloe, with whom he continues to associate in the old way.

Chloe's beauty and charm bring many suitors, who ask her of her foster-parents. Daphnis, sorely alarmed because of his poverty, is told by the Nymphs in a dream that on the shore he will find a purse of three thousand drachmas, cast ashore out of the ship of the young Methymnaeans. Securing the money, he boldly presents himself as a rich man before Dryas, who promises to give him Chloe as his bride. Daphnis' foster-father Lamon, who knows nothing of the three thousand drachmas, agrees to the match, but the parties must await the consent of their master in Mytilene. Daphnis hurries to Chloe with the good news, and gives her a sweet-scented apple, plucked from the highest branch of the tree, as a token of his troth.

Towards the end of the summer the rustics receive news that the visit of their master Dionysophanes is at hand. Lamon prepares a beautiful garden against his coming, but this is destroyed by Lampis, one of Chloe's rejected suitors. Astylus, the son of Dionysophanes, arrives before his father, and pardons the terrified Lamon. Dionysophanes and his wife Clearista arrive with a large retinue. Gnathon, the 'parasite' of Astylus, asks Astylus to give him Daphnis as a present, and Astylus in turn begs his father to give him Daphnis as his own servant. Since there is grave danger that Daphnis will be sent to Mytilene as a slave, Lamon confesses that he is not really Daphnis' father. Then follow the story of the finding of Daphnis, and the exhibition of the tokens. On seeing these, Dionysophanes and Clearista recognize in Daphnis their own son, whom they had exposed in infancy because he was their fourth child and they were unwilling to divide their fortune among so many. But meanwhile two of the other children have died, and now they rejoice to have him back.

Chloe, in the meantime, thinks herself deserted by Daphnis, and is disconsolate. Lampis, the rejected suitor, abducts her forcibly, but she is soon rescued by a party under Gnathon, who hopes thus to be restored to the favour of Daphnis. Dryas now tells the master how Chloe was found. Dionysophanes agrees to her marriage with Daphnis, and carries her and Daphnis back with him to Mytilene. Prompted in a dream by the Nymphs, he gives a feast to the most distinguished citizens of Mytilene, and shows to his guests the tokens found with Chloe. These are recognized by the wealthy Megacles, who acknowledges Chloe as his daughter. He had exposed her in infancy because of his poverty, but now, become rich, welcomes her back. At the wish of Daphnis and Chloe, the wedding took place in the country, before their beloved grotto of the Nymphs. And in the country they lived happily most of their days, serving the Nymphs and Pan and Eros.

Such, then, is the story of Daphnis and Chloe, the love-story of a goatherd and a shepherdess, the sole ancient example of a union of the romance with the pastoral. But although, as pastoral, the *Daphnis and Chloe* stands alone, it has elements which are shared by the other Greek novels. I name first the element of adventure. The abduction of Chloe by Lampis and her rescue by Gnathon and his party; the encounters with the men of Methymna; the incursion of the Tyrian pirates—these episodes, though skilfully enough introduced, are not essential to the development of the plot, and are on that account perhaps the more significant. They are imported into the narrative, not merely be-çause 'the course of true love never did run smooth', but also, and primarily, in order to satisfy that fondness for tales of adventure which is inherent even in the most home-biding and peace-loving of humankind. You may trace the tale of adventure in Greek literature, if you please, back to Homer, assenting to the view that Homer is the universal spring; or you may regard it, in the novel, as owing something to Oriental contacts; and yet, as we survey the tale of adventure in its various ancient forms, I doubt whether we need look beyond the simple fact that the world has always been full of Desdemonas, male as well as female, who 'to hear would . . . seriously incline' whenever a tale is told

> Of moving accidents by flood and field,
> Of hair-breadth scapes i' the imminent deadly breach,
> Of being taken by the insolent foe
> And sold to slavery.

However this may be, adventure became a traditional and constant ingredient in the Greek novel.

Longus, then, was conforming to tradition in adding an element of adventure; and in part, the adventures thus added to his narrative are of traditional kinds. 'Again pirates and the sea! Again I am a prisoner!' exclaims Anthea in Xenophon of Ephesus.[1] Poor girl, the reader wouldn't have been happy without them. You will meet either pirates or brigands, or both, in Xenophon of Ephesus, in Chariton, in Heliodorus, in Achilles Tatius; we shall encounter them, too, in the

---

[1] Xen. Eph. iii. 8 πάλιν, ἔφησε, λῃσταὶ καὶ θάλαττα, πάλιν αἰχμάλωτος ἐγώ.

Golden Ass of Apuleius, which, though written in Latin, is derived in great part from a Greek original. In fact, they also are among the stock properties of the writer of romances. Their leaders, as Dunlop, in his *History of Prose Fiction*, has observed, 'are frequently the second characters, and occupy the part of the unsuccessful lovers of the heroine; but are not always painted as endued with any peculiar bad qualities, or as exciting horror in the other persons of the work'. Thus Chaereas, in the *Leucippe and Clitophon*, appears as a very decent fellow, who even does Leucippe the service of curing her madness, until, having fallen in love with her, he brings his pirate band to carry her off. In the same romance Menelaus and Satyrus, staunch friends of hero and heroine, join the brigands for a time. In Xenophon of Ephesus the robber Hippothous, when plying his trade, is as ruthless as you please; but the blameless hero associates with him on amicable terms and even, it seems, goes marauding with him; and in the end Hippothous settles at Ephesus as the dear friend of the reunited Habrocomes and Anthea. After all, piracy and brigandage were tolerably respectable professions in the early days of Greece, and even later. This we are told, for example, by Thucydides in the fifth chapter of his first book. Up to the time of Pompey, in the first century before Christ, the people of Cilicia lived largely by piracy, and no doubt neither regarded themselves, nor were by others regarded, as criminals and outcasts. You will remember the old man, *Corycium senem*, whose prodigies of gardening at Tarentum are described so delightfully by Virgil in the Fourth Georgic. He was a Cilician, probably one of those who, after Pompey's successful campaign against the

pirates, beat their cutlasses into pruning-hooks. As
pirate, let us hope, he had been

> the mildest-mannered man
> That ever scuttled ship or cut a throat;

as gardener, he was the champion of Italy. Probably
the pirate and the brigand found their place in fiction
when they were realities to be reckoned with in everyday life; they maintained it, because they provided
welcome thrills for the slippered reader in his arm-
chair, and because, viewed from a distance, they were
not without a tincture of the heroic. Indeed, the heroism has sometimes been real enough: witness Drake,
who had more than a little of the pirate in him, and yet
is justly numbered among the most heroic figures in
our nation's story. But even where, as in the *Daphnis
and Chloe*, the pirates are no heroes, but only naughty
rogues practising a lawless trade, their presence is
further justified, if it is the business of a novelist to
entertain, by the attractiveness of the lawless even for
the most law-abiding spirits. Note, in our own time,
the vogue of the detective-novel and the 'thriller'.

A second point of contact between the *Daphnis and
Chloe* and other Greek novels is found in the supernatural element, in the intervention of Powers that are
divine, or at any rate superhuman. Eros, the winged
god of love, appears before old Philetas and tells how
he has chosen Daphnis and Chloe to be his favourites;
the Nymphs twice comfort Daphnis in a dream; Pan,
chief god of the herdsfolk, rescues Chloe from her captors. All these, you note, are members of that band of
minor deities, usually well-disposed, who stand in more
intimate relation to humanity than the high host of

Olympian gods. Yet other writers of romances do not scruple to introduce greater divinities. In *Leucippe and Clitophon*, for instance, Zeus himself and Artemis and Aphrodite intervene, through omen or dream. But there is no need to multiply examples: here once more we have a regular constituent of the Greek novels. It is not likely that any but the most sceptical and sophisticated of ancient readers found fault with this intervention of deities in the affairs of men, or felt that there was any inartistic violation of probability. Even the sceptic was prepared for it by an acquaintance with Greek poetic fiction, which for more than ten centuries, from Homer onwards, had expatiated in a mythic world in which gods conversed familiarly with mankind. Greeks even of this late age, and Romans too, were steeped in the ancient myths. These novels themselves go far to prove it; but perhaps the most striking evidence is that furnished by the remains of Graeco-Roman pictorial art. In Pompeii, to mention the most notable example, there is scarcely a house which does not, or did not, bear upon its walls fresco-paintings the subjects of which, in the main, are drawn from the ancient tales of gods and heroes: scenes from *Iliad* or *Odyssey*; the story of Artemis and Actaeon; of Orpheus and Eurydice; of Pentheus; of Medea; of Perseus and Andromeda; and so forth. Children were born and grew up among these, and absorbed them into their mental and spiritual being, not otherwise than children of later ages absorbed Bible and hagiology from contemplation of the mosaics and paintings and windows in Christian churches.

More particularly might Longus venture to make the rustic divinities play a part. It is said that when the

Golden Age wore to an end and the gods withdrew in displeasure from mankind, they tarried longest among the country-folk, in whom uncorrupted simplicity and virtue longest survived. It is a matter of historical fact that belief in the old gods was strongest and most enduring among the rustics: did not they, the *pagani* (whence our 'pagans'), continue to worship the old gods even after Christianity had triumphed in the cities? Moreover, the peculiar deities of the rustics were conceived, not as living apart among the Olympians, but as haunting with their bodily presence field and pasture, vineyard woodland and stream. If, then, there were gods, and gods took thought for mankind, who more likely to encounter them than the rustic, firm of belief and innocent of life, who had these very gods for neighbours? In the rustic and idyllic setting of the *Daphnis and Chloe*, Eros and Pan and the Nymphs are not incongruous.

All of these divinities are friendly to the young lovers, and Eros plays a part in determining their life and love which is comparable with that played by Fortune in *Leucippe and Clitophon*. But though in the *Daphnis and Chloe* divinities sometimes appear in person, in it, as in the other romances, they usually act through omens and dreams, faith in which was almost universal and itself implied some belief in supernatural powers. The omen is a direct sending from gods, but the dream also, as Homer said, comes from above. Both omen and dream would be accepted by an ancient reader without question and as a matter of course; and neither of them, in Longus and his fellow novelists, needs any apology.

Certain forms of ornament, also, Longus shares with his fellows; but he chooses them, and weaves them into the fabric of his story, with a more finished art and a keener sense of propriety. Let me offer a single illustration. Achilles Tatius introduces a picture of the rape of Philomel as an omen of the peril that threatens Leucippe. No more is either necessary or legitimate. But he then describes the picture in detail and, as if this were not enough, appends a long relation of the myth of Tereus and Procne and Philomel, for which he can devise no better excuse than that Leucippe, being a woman, is fond of stories.[1] It is plain that the transformation of Philomel into a swallow, Tereus into a hoopoe, and Procne into a nightingale, and all the rest of the myth, have no relevance to the fortunes of Leucippe and Clitophon, but constitute a 'purple patch' stitched to the narrative by the loosest and most conspicuous of threads. But when Longus similarly relates the myth of a woman transformed into a bird, he chooses a rustic myth, told of just such a simple herdsmaid as Chloe herself, and makes the narrative spring naturally from an experience of his hero and heroine.[2] Let me read it to you in Angell Daye's beautiful paraphrase:

'Shortly hereupon it befell that a certain Ringdove sitting in a grove hard by, began to sing, in whose song Chloe taking great delight, demaunded of Daphnis the reason thereof, whereupon the gentle Goatheard desirous of her utmost satisfaction, began to recompt unto her, this storie following.

'There was (my dere) sayd hee, in times passed, a young damosell fayre of shape, and in the prime of her age, bewtifull as your selfe, who keeping her cattell upon these pastures, had right excellent skill, both to sing and playe delicately. Her beastes had pleasure in her tunes, and so delightfull was

[1] Ach. Tat. v. 5 φιλόμυθον γάρ πως τὸ τῶν γυναικῶν γένος.　　[2] i. 27.

the sound of her voyce and pipe, that shee governed them at pleasure, and was able to drawe them whether she would.

'This beautifull *Nymphe* sitting under a statelie Pine, having her head crowned with the leaves thereof, one daye happened to sing a song in the honour of Pan, wherewith her beastes began so earnestly to be enclined, as that they drewe them close to her soundes. Neere unto her was there likewyse keeping of Cattell a certaine young youth, freshe and froolicke as her selfe, who right well handled his pipe, and could thereon playe manie deintie ditties. One daie amongst the rest, with intent to shewe that his comming[1] was not bad, hee tooke his pipe in hande, and thereon in disdaine of the *Nymphe*, plaied so sweetly and melodiously, as that with the over-pleasing sounde thereof, hee drewe from her eight of her fayrest beastes, pursuing the sweetnesse of his Pipe, doe what shee could, and made them to joyne to his companie, where-with the poore wenche vexed for griefe and intollerable dispite, to see hir flockes so muche to be diminished, and chiefly also, that she was thus overcome in hir own cunning, tooke so great a griefe of the same, as that shee praied the gods, and they vouchsafed to change hir into a foule, rather than any more wyth such infamie to returne to hir dwelling. This performed, and she, as you see, being made a bird of the mountaine, in accustomed sort, followeth up and downe, plaining hir ill hap and losse of hir beasts, whome she seeketh, being thus as she was unluckily overcome, and sing-

---

[1] i.e. 'coming', as elsewhere in Daye. The phrase seems to mean that the youth, in order to show that he came with peaceful intent and had no evil design on the person of the damsel, took up his pipe and began to play. There is nothing of this in Amyot's version (1559), of which Daye's work is a free paraphrase. Even the pipe is of Daye's invention, for in Amyot (and the Greek) the youth sings. Amyot has: 'Or y auoit il au pres de là vn ieune garson qui gardoit des beufz, il estoit beau & chantoit bien aussi, vn jour pour mòstrer qu'il sçavoit autant de chanter còme elle, il se mist à chanter si doulcement, et si mélodieusement qu'il attira à luy huict des plus belles vaches. . . .' For this transcript of Amyot I am indebted to the kindness of Professor A. W. Boase, of the University of Glasgow.

ing as she was woont to doe reteineth yet some part of hir
auntient tunes and sorowfull complainings.'

Of elements common to the *Daphnis and Chloe* and the
other novels, there remains the most important of all,
namely, love. For the *Daphnis and Chloe* also belongs to
the class of *erotica*, owning love for its principal theme.
Whatever else in the Greek novels may be derived ultimately from Homer, this at any rate owes nothing to
Homeric influence. The love of man and maid, of
wife and husband, of parent and child—love in all its
forms is as old as mankind. Yet in Homer it receives
the scantiest notice. Since he, like Sophocles, 'saw life
steadily and saw it whole', he could not fail to recognize
love, and even passion, among the virtues and the
frailties of humanity; but he regards neither as being,
even potentially, the serious business of human life.
Else he would not have touched so lightly on the love
of Trojan Paris for Argive Helen,

> the face that launched a thousand ships
> And burnt the topless towers of Ilium,

nor made enamoured Circe address Ulysses with the
laconic bluntness of a Potiphar's wife. Though later
poets in their several domains—lyric, elegiac, dramatic, pastoral, even epic—assign to love a juster and
ampler range, it remained for the novelists to cultivate
a new literary mode, planned almost on the epic scale,
but using prose as its medium, in which love was made
the essential fabric of the work. At their worst, they
commit extravagances and absurdities that would
provoke the mirth of a guileless and sentimental
schoolgirl, or indulge a frankness that would bring a

blush to the cheek of a Freudian psycho-analyst; at their best, they exhibit a knowledge of the human heart, a grace of sentiment and an artistry of expression that are not altogether unworthy of the great name of Greek.

In his treatment of love, Longus, in spite of his general superiority, is not quite free from the faults of the species. Judged by the standards of real life, the simplicity of his hero and heroine is overdone, even to the point of caricature; and there are two or three episodes, arising from this, which have brought him under suspicion of pandering to a depraved taste. It has been said that if Daphnis and Chloe are innocent, Longus himself is not. But I myself incline to a more charitable opinion. To these sophist-novelists no subject is under a ban if only it give them scope for the elaboration of their art: witness, as notable examples, the debate with which Achilles Tatius concludes his second book, and the circumstances of the heroine's birth in Heliodorus. Not only is frankness, in the Greek view, compatible with decency, but in Longus' imagined world the canons of reality are no more valid than in the world of myth, where no one would think of applying them.

After asserting that the *Daphnis and Chloe* differs from the rest of the Greek novels, I have spent much time in pointing out its affinities to them. Let me now explain wherein it is unique. I repeat, then, that it is the only example in Greek of the pastoral romance.

The love of country life had found some expression in Greek literature even in the old days of the small city-state. You will find it, for instance, in the comedies of Aristophanes, as when Trygaeus, in the *Peace*, sings

> Think of all the thousand pleasures,
> Comrades, which to Peace we owe,
> All the life of ease and comfort
> Which she gave us long ago:
> Figs and olives, wine and myrtles,
> Luscious fruits preserved and dried,
> Banks of fragrant violets, blowing
> By the crystal fountain's side;
> Scenes for which our hearts are yearning,
> Joys that we have missed so long,—
> Comrades, here is Peace returning,
> Greet her back with dance and song.[1]

But a new era begins with the conquests of Alexander the Great in the latter half of the fourth century before Christ. With the establishment of an empire over the eastern part of the Hellenic world and even over non-Hellenic lands in Asia and Africa, Hellas ceased to be an aggregation of independent and self-contained city-states, each with a small territory of its own. The Successors of Alexander, from their several capitals, ruled over dominions which were wider by far than any ruled by Greeks in earlier days, and that included within their boundaries many towns. The Hellenic Age was succeeded by the Hellenistic. The change in political and social conditions thus brought about is accurately reflected in Hellenistic literature, which is in the main a literature written by dwellers in the great capital cities such as Alexandria.

---

[1] Aristophanes, *Peace*, 571 ff. (Rogers's translation).

When the enterprising burglar's not a-burgling,

sings the Sergeant of Police in *The Pirates of Penzance*,

When the cut-throat isn't occupied in crime,
He loves to hear the little brook a-gurgling,
And listen to the merry village chime.

Whether one's occupation be burglary or business—or scholarship—the restlessness, the artificiality, the complexity of life in a great town breed an eager longing for the peace and beauty and simplicity of the country. For the phenomenon is not peculiar to the age or to the countries of which I am now speaking. The same motive impelled Horace to escape from 'the smoke and wealth and din of Rome' and retire to his farm on the Digentia, the same sends the undergraduate out to his vacation camp in some mountain glen.

Thus it was that in the Hellenistic Age the country, as never before, came into its own, and nowhere more than in poetry. It was in this age that the Pastoral, as a poetic form, had its origin and attained its highest development. The inventor seems to have been Philetas of Cos, whose name appears in the *Daphnis and Chloe* as the name of the old herdsman who instructs the two children in the nature of love: perhaps, as Legrand suggested, a tacit acknowledgement that the 'bucolic masquerade', in whatever form, is derived ultimately from him.[1] But I need not remind you that the greatest master of the poetic pastoral was Theocritus. His Idylls, set for the greater part in a Sicilian landscape, are not the less poetry of a high order because they present, as Cholmeley said, 'not a sketch of country

[1] Legrand, *Étude sur Théocrite*, p. 155, quoted by Cholmeley in the Introduction to his edition of Theocritus.

men and manners, but a refined imitation thereof in pseudo-shepherds and pseudo-neatherds'.[1]

A new poetic type was thus forged: the bucolic idyll, which dealt exclusively with life in the country and the beauties of nature; but apart from this, 'nature' now occupies an ampler place in poetry generally. Finally, descriptions of nature and of country life become favourite exercises of the schools, and are found still to persist among those sophist-rhetoricians of a later time of whom, as we have seen, Longus was one. Let me illustrate this aspect of the *Daphnis and Chloe* by quoting two specimens. The first is from the twenty-third chapter of Book I:

'For now the cooler spring was ended, and the Summer was ended, and the Autumn was come on, and all things were got to their highest flourishing *akme* and vigour; the trees with their fruits, the fields with standing Corn. Sweet then, was the singing of the Grasshoppers; sweet was the odour of the fruits; and not unpleasant, the very bleating of the sheep. A man would have thought that the very rivers by their gentle gliding away, did sing; and that the softer gales of wind, did play, and whistle on the pines; that the Cattel, as languishing with love, lay down and slumbered on the ground.'

The second is from the third chapter of Book III:

'And now Winter was come on, a winter more bitter than war, to Daphnis and Chloe. For on a suddain there fell a great Snow which blinded all the paths, stopt up all wayes, and shut up all the Shepherds and Colones. The very Torrents were frozen and glazed with Chrystal. The hedges and trees lookt as if they had bin clipt and cropt; and there was nothing to be seen but stumps. All the ground was hood-

---

[1] Cholmeley, l.c., p. 12, 1st edition.

winkt up, but that which lay upon the fountains and the rills. And therefore no man drove out his flocks to pasture, or did so much as come to the door, but about the Cock's crowing made their fires nosehigh; and some spun flax, some Tarpaulin for the Sea; others, with all their Sophistry, made gins, and nets, and traps for birds. . . . But all things are pervious to Love, even Fire, Water, and Scythian Snowes. Therefore, plodding through, he came up to the Cottage, and when he had shook the Snow from his thighs, he set his snares, and prickt his lime-twiggs. Then he sate down, and thought of nothing carefully, but of Chloe and the birds.'

I quoted those two passages from George Thornley's translation.[1] Thornley has all the felicity of the great Elizabethan translators, though his version was made fifty-four years after the death of Elizabeth. And although, being a sounder scholar, at any rate in Latin,[2] he will give you a more faithful translation than any of them, you must not expect to find in him any slavish literalness. You will not take it amiss if a 'lump of meat' becomes a 'shoulder of mutton'; if 'a male child' is improved into 'a jolly boy'; if the simple 'thirsty' is heightened into 'almost choked for want of drink', 'they lit a big fire' into 'they made their fires nosehigh'; and so forth. Although Thornley takes many such liberties with his author's text, he takes far fewer than most Elizabethan translators, for instance than Angell Daye; he is not apt to err through mere ignorance; and he reproduces the spirit of his original, in the main, with remarkable fidelity.

To me it seems beyond question that the *Daphnis and Chloe* and some, at least, of the other romances, owe a debt also to the New Attic Comedy, the Comedy imi-

[1] From a reprint, with decorations by John Austen, published by Geoffrey Bles, 1925.　[2] He made more use of Jungermann's Latin than of Longus' Greek.

tated by the Latin comic dramatists. This was a comedy of manners, in which the persons of the play were types rather than individuals. The types are not very many: the puritanical father; the prodigal son; the slave who plots for the young master against the old; the courtesan; the pander; the 'parasite', ever scheming for a meal; the braggart soldier; and so on. There was a stock list of names for characters of the several types: the same names for characters of the same type are sometimes used by several dramatists, and even several times by the same dramatist. The allocation of name to type was invariable, with only one known exception:[1] Davus is always a slave; Sophrona a nurse; Phaedria a young man; Sostrata a matron; Chremes an old man; and so on. Accordingly, when in the *Daphnis and Chloe* we find a nurse Sophrone and a parasite Gnathon,[2] we may be sure of direct derivation from the New Comedy. In *Leucippe and Clitophon*, Satyrus, the unscrupulous but devoted slave of Clitophon, is a type taken directly from the New Comedy. Of the New Comedy, again, as of the romances, the troubles of two young lovers are among the staple themes. Lastly, the exposure of children with tokens, and their ultimate recognition by means of these, were a device so commonly used in the New Attic Comedy, though not altogether restricted to that form of drama, that one may reasonably conclude that Longus and Heliodorus,[3]

---

[1] In the *Eunuch* of Terence, imitated from the Greek of Menander, Chremes is the name of a *young* man who at his first appearance shows notable sobriety.

[2] As in Terence's *Eunuchus*; there is a nurse Sophrona in both *Eunuchus* and *Phormio*.

[3] *Theagenes and Chariclea*, x. 14. That Heliodorus had a commonplace of drama (if not of comedy) in mind becomes evident when Chariclea's father, King Hydaspes, is made to say (x. 12) that her claim to be his daughter is like a scene in a stage play.

both of whom use it, derived it from Comedy rather than from some other source.

Regarded from whatever point of view, the *Daphnis and Chloe* is the best of the Greek novels. Although its theme, the birth of love in boy and girl and the ripening of this love to full maturity while the two young people work and play together on their sequestered Lesbian pastures—though its theme, I say, the origin, development, and realization of an emotion, presented unusual difficulties to the writer in these early days of the Romance, yet the story marches in a steady and orderly progress to its appointed goal. Achilles Tatius, as we saw, describes the growth of love and a brief wooing, but thereafter conforms to type. In these romances, other than the *Daphnis and Chloe*, we meet at the outset, or soon after, a pair of lovers who have diagnosed their ailment; who are prepared, in fact, for marriage, if they are not already married. These are parted and plagued by an unkind fortune. The author then conducts them through a long series of adventures by land and sea, until at last they are reunited in happy wedlock. In *Leucippe and Clitophon* and the rest, adventure follows adventure in a sequence which threatens to be interminable:

> It takes up about eighty thousand lines,
> A thing imagination boggles at:
> And might, odds-bobs, sir! in judicious hands,
> Extend from here to Mesopotamy.

If the author does not aim at dramatic unity, if he is satisfied merely to string together episodes which have no necessary logical or developmental relation to one another, until his romance attains the desired length, he may produce an entertaining novel; but he will certainly incur the censure which Aristotle pronounced on episodic Tragedy. 'The "episodic"', he says, 'are the worst of all plots and actions. By an "episodic" plot I mean one in which the succession of episodes is not determined either by likelihood or by necessity. Bad poets compose such plays because they cannot help it, good poets because the actors want them.'[1]

Longus does not eschew the episode, though he dispenses with the element of travel. But his episodes, while appearing to interrupt the flow of the story, actually serve an artistic purpose, as Croiset observed. Take, as an example, the episode of Daphnis' fall into the pit which had been dug to catch a wolf. Chloe's fear throws her into a flutter which makes her receptive of new emotions. She then stands by while the rescued Daphnis cleanses himself from the mire that has befouled his body, and the sight of his beauty sets the spark to love. Again, the Dorkon episode furnishes Chloe with the means of saving Daphnis from the pirates; while the incursions of the pirates and of the men from Methymna intensify the love of hero and heroine by making each in turn suffer the pangs of ravishment and separation. Whereas Tatius might be a hack-novelist producing month by month his instalment of a serial; not knowing, on the delivery of his instalment, what he is to write for the next; sure only that he must be both sentimental and 'sensational', and that at the end he must exhibit love triumphant—Longus, on the other hand, has schemed his plot as a whole, and has made cause follow cause, if not to an inevitable, at any rate to a probable issue. There are improbabilities in

[1] Aristotle, *Poetics*, ix.

Longus, no doubt. But if we accept his postulates—the more (or less) than human simplicity of hero and heroine; the possibility of divine intervention in the affairs of mortals; the magic power of the pastoral pipes—there is nothing in Longus that seriously outrages common sense. There is no disembowelled heroine coming to life again, as in Achilles Tatius;[1] no crucified hero, as in Xenophon of Ephesus,[2] falling with his cross into the Nile and thus floating down the river to ultimate safety.

Longus, being a sophist, must needs sophisticate, but even his sophistication of simple things can be charming. Listen to this, from the twenty-fifth chapter of the first book. Daphnis is watching Chloe while she sleeps:

'How sweet', he murmurs, 'are her sleeping eyes, how sweet the breath of her mouth! Not so sweet the scent of apples nor of the coppices. But I am afraid to kiss her: for her kiss stings my heart and makes me mad, like new honey. And I shrink, too, lest by kissing I awaken her. Oh, the chattering cicadas! They will not let her sleep for their great noise. Nay, and the goats make a clatter with their horns as they fight: oh, but the wolves must be more cowardly than foxes, that they have not ravished these goats away!'

And listen to this, Lamon's lament for the ruined garden, from the eighth chapter of the fourth book:

'Alas, the rosary, how it hath been broken down! Alas, the violary, how it hath been trampled! Alas, the hyacinth and the narcissus, that some villain hath dug up! Spring will come, but they will not blossom; 'twill be summer, but they will not reach their prime; autumn, but these will make no one a garland. And didst not even thou, lord Dionysus, pity these poor flowers, by which thou didst dwell and on

---

[1] iii. 15 ff.   [2] iv. 2.

which thou didst look, of which I often wove a garland for thee and was glad?'

I have read you these two passages in my own rendering, for Thornley has further embellished an already highly embellished original. The point that I wish to make is this. In essentials, the sentiment is sound. Your genuine rustic may watch in love and admiration over his sleeping beauty and execrate the sounds that may disturb her slumber; and he may surely lament the wanton destruction of the loveliness that the labour of his hands has wrought; but these simple sentiments are cast in a rhetorical mould which reveals in every detail the artifices of the sophist:

> Alas, the rosary, how it hath been broken down!
> Alas, the violary, how it hath been trampled!

And again:

> Spring will come, but they will not blossom;
> 'Twill be summer, but they will not reach their prime.

It is the thought of the rustic, but the ornament of the rhetorician. Still, much greater men have done worse. Read *Rasselas*, for instance, and marvel at the spectacle of an elephant juggling with an egg. There is nothing ponderous about Longus. He is rhetorical, he is affected, even to the point of travesty: but in a tale of two rustic innocents, what travesty more venial than this, from homespun into daintiest lawn?

Daphnis and Chloe was known in Elizabethan England through the French version of Amyot, published in 1559, and the English adaptation by Angell Daye, published in 1587, both of which preceded the first printed edition of the Greek text, which appeared at Florence in 1598. Amyot's version, after nearly four centuries, is still, in Courier's revision, widely current in France. Angell Daye was not acquainted with the Greek, but produced a free adaptation of Amyot, with which he incorporated, under the name of *The Shepherd's Holiday*, a masque in honour of Queen Elizabeth. His book exists now, it seems, in a single copy; but it may be read in a reprint which was issued in 1890 with an introduction by Joseph Jacobs. Not many Elizabethan Englishmen had Greek enough, or even Latin enough, to be able to dispense with a translator's aid. But the Elizabethan Age was an age of great translators, among whom Daye occupies a respectable place, though he does not rank with the greatest. One would look to them in vain for accurate scholarship, to which indeed they did not pretend; but they could give to a translation, even to a translation made, as so many were, at second hand, the appearance and value of an original. This, indeed, was their design: no mere scholarly *tour de force*, but the enrichment of the native literature by the transplantation of the ancient masterpieces now newly recovered. Not all the works they translated would now be esteemed masterpieces; not all the novels, for instance. But, as Gaselee remarks, in the sixteenth century literary appetites were unjaded.[1] The rediscovered treasures that were thus made accessible were read eagerly, and furnished even the greatest writers of the time both with themes for the exercise of their own genius and with models for imitation.

Of the Elizabethans, Robert Greene was steeped in the three romances known to his generation, namely

[1] *Appendix on the Greek Novel*, in the Loeb edition of *Daphnis and Chloe*, p. 403.

those of Longus, Heliodorus, and Achilles Tatius.[1] In his *Menaphon* he outdoes his sources in absurdities. Part of the pastoral detail derived by Greene from Longus and used by him in his *Pandosto* is borrowed by Shakespeare and used over again in *The Winter's Tale*. Dr. Wolff, in his *Greek Romances in Elizabethan Fiction*,[2] draws attention to a probable example of direct borrowing by Shakespeare from Longus, namely the incident of the hunt in Act III, Scene iii, of *The Winter's Tale*, apparently derived from the incident of the Methymnaeans' hunt in the *Daphnis and Chloe*.[3] In that scene Antigonus exposes the baby Perdita on a lonely shore in Bohemia. Shakespeare must now bring his Shepherd down to the shore to find her, and must kill Antigonus to prevent him from telling the story of the exposure. He therefore introduces the hunt. In the *Daphnis and Chloe* the young men from Methymna land for a day's recreation. They go hunting, and so frighten the herds that they leave their pastures and go down to the shore. Here was Shakespeare's solution. He brings in his Shepherd, searching for strayed sheep on the shore:

'I would', says the Shepherd, 'I would there were no age between ten and three and twenty, or that youth would sleep out the rest: for there is nothing (in the betweene) but getting wenches with child, wronging the Auncientry, stealing, fighting, hearke you now: would any but these boylde-braines of nineteene, and two and twenty hunt this weather? They have scarr'd away two of my best Sheepe, which I feare the Wolfe will sooner finde than the Maister; if anywhere I have them, 'tis by the sea-side, browzing of Ivy.'

As he looks for the sheep, he finds the child. To him

---

[1] For particulars of this, and amplification of what follows, see Dr. Wolff's *Greek Romances in Elizabethan Fiction*.   [2] pp. 452 ff.   [3] ii. 12 ff.

presently enters the Clown, who tells him how he has seen the ship wrecked by the storm, and Antigonus eaten by a bear that had been driven down to the shore by the huntsmen:

> CLOWN: To see how the Beare tore out his shoulder-bone, how he cride to mee for helpe, and said his name was Antigonus, a Nobleman: But to make an end of the Ship, to see how the Sea flap-dragon'd it: but first, how the poore soules roared, and the sea mock'd them: and how the poore Gentleman roared, and the Beare mock'd him, both roaring lowder than the sea, or weather.
>
> SHEPHERD: Name of mercy, when was this boy?
>
> CLOWN: Now, now: I have not wink'd since I saw these sights: the men are not yet cold under water, nor the Beare halfe din'd on the Gentleman: he's at it now.

Even the dramatically convenient shipwreck in this scene may have been suggested by Longus, who makes a gale rise and wreck the ship of the Methymnaeans after the goats have gnawed her adrift.

If we concede that these correspondences are not likely to be accidental, we have in this scene an interesting and typical example of Shakespeare's use of borrowed material. His borrowing is of seed which germinates in a fertile brain and springs up to new and independent life. If he borrows here and there from the Greek romances, he does not, in the strictest sense of the term, imitate them. For imitation we must look, among his contemporaries, in men of lesser genius: in Greene, for instance, and Lyly, and Sir Philip Sidney.

To pass from matter to style, the affectations of the Elizabethan Euphuists are in great part a reflection of the affectations of Greek Romance. I quote, as a single example, part of a dialogue between Agenor and

Eriphila, in the *Menaphon*, on the love of the Sun and the Marigold:

'Not so, sweete wife, answered *Agenor*, but the comparison holdeth in this, that as the Marigold resembleth the Sunne both in colour and forme, so each mans wife ought everie way to be the image of her husband, framing her countenance to smile, when she sees him disposed to mirth; and contrariwise her eyes to teares, he being surcharged with melancholy: and as the Marigold displaieth the orient ornaments of her beautie to the resplendant viewe of none but her lover *Hyperion*, so ought not a woman of modestie lay open the allurements of her face to anie but her espoused pheere; in whose absence like the Marigold in the absence of the Sunne, she ought to shut up her dores, and solemnize continuall night, till her husband, her sunne, making a happie return, unsealeth her silence with the joy of his sight.'

That might have been taken straight from one of the old Greek novels.

Longus invented the pastoral romance, and his influence is found throughout the pastorals of the modern European literatures: already, perhaps, at the end of the fifteenth century, in the *Arcadia* of the 'Neapolitan Virgil' Jacopo Sannazaro; in the *Aminta* of Tasso, in the *Astrée* of D'Urfé, in the *Gentle Shepherd* of Ramsay, in the *Paul et Virginie* of Saint-Pierre, and in other writings almost countless.

III

THE 'SATIRICON'

FROM Achilles Tatius and Longus we pass to Petronius and Apuleius, and find that in the novel, if in little else, the Romans not only equalled but even excelled the Greeks. In discussing the *Leucippe and Clitophon* and the *Daphnis and Chloe* it was necessary, at times, to exchange the part of expositor and critic for that of apologist; but the *Satiricon* and the *Golden Ass*, considered as works of art, need no defence.

In the *Daphnis and Chloe* we encountered the sole example, in antiquity, of a union of the romance with the pastoral; in the work of Petronius we shall find the romance in combination with satire. In this respect, as in many others, the *Satiricon* is both unique, in the ancient literatures, and characteristically Roman. Everybody is familiar with Quintilian's boast *Satira quidem tota nostra est*. Satire, Quintilian claimed, unlike other forms of literature, was not of Greek origin but an independent creation of Rome. The earliest *satura* was a medley, as the name itself denotes: a medley either of different kinds of verse or else of intermingled verse and prose. Lucilius, in the latter half of the second century before Christ, after experimenting with a variety of metres, finally chose a single metre, the dactylic hexameter, as the appropriate vehicle. He further used *satura*[1] for the purposes of polemic, and so made the name *satura*, for the first time, connote 'satire' in the sense that the word has borne ever since, namely, a censorious description and criticism of human

---

[1] Later, the spelling *satira* becomes current.

K

affairs. His example was followed more or less closely by Horace and Persius and Juvenal. But the medley did not die out altogether. Varro, a contemporary of Cicero in the first century before Christ, wrote, in vast bulk, what he called 'Menippean Satires', a work partly in prose and partly in verse, of which some hundreds of short fragments are still extant. The name 'Menippean' indicated his indebtedness to the Cynic philosopher Menippus who, in the third century before Christ, had written humorously on philosophical themes. In the time of Nero, beyond which we need not go, there appeared two works in the same tradition. Seneca wrote the *Apocolocyntosis*, which is satire pure and simple; and Petronius wrote the *Satiricon* (some think that it should be called *Satirae*), which is not true satire but a satirical novel cast in the Menippean mould. That is the work to which we now turn our attention.

There is no sound reason for doubting that the author of this remarkable work was that Gaius[1] Petronius whose death under Nero, in the year 66 after Christ, is recorded by the historian Tacitus in the sixteenth book of the *Annals*. In the seventeenth chapter of that book Tacitus mentions the death of four eminent Romans, of whom one was Petronius. Then in the eighteenth chapter he writes:

'In telling of C. Petronius I must recall briefly his earlier career. His day would be passed in sleep, his night in the duties and pleasures of life. As industry advances others to fame, so had indolence advanced him; and he was regarded not as a debauchee and prodigal, like most of those who

---

[1] Tacitus calls him Gaius, the Elder Pliny and Plutarch call him Titus. Even a contemporary can err in such matters, as Wilamowitz, for instance, in an appreciation of Jebb called him Sir Robert Jebb, a slip perpetuated in the reprint of his *Kleine Schriften*, i, p. 461.

waste their substance, but as a man of tutored voluptuous-
ness. And the more unrestrained were his words and deeds,
the more suggestive of a certain recklessness of self, with the
greater approval were they interpreted as evidence of simplicity. Yet as governor of Bithynia, and soon afterwards as
consul, he showed himself vigorous and an able man of
affairs. Then, slipping back into vice, or in simulation of
vice, he was received into the select company of Nero's
intimates as *elegantiae arbiter*, "arbiter of taste", determining
which of the pleasures of superabundance should be approved
by the Emperor. He thus incurred the jealousy of Tigellinus,
who regarded him as a rival, his superior in the science of
pleasure. Tigellinus therefore applied himself to the Emperor's cruelty, his ruling passion, charging Petronius with
having been the friend of Scaevinus. He bribed a slave to
give information, made defence impossible, and imprisoned
the greater part of his household.

'It chanced that just then Caesar was visiting Campania,
and Petronius, having travelled as far as Cumae, was being
detained there. He endured no longer the postponement of
fear or hope. Yet he did not banish life in haste. Having
cut his veins, he would bind them up and open them again
as he pleased. Meanwhile he would speak to his friends, but
not on serious topics nor to make a parade of fortitude; and
he would listen to them regaling him, not with disquisitions
on immortality nor with the doctrines of philosophers, but
with light poems and ribald verses. On some of his slaves
he bestowed his bounty, on others a flogging. He dined and
he slept, so that his death, though forced, should seem to be
natural. Even in his will he did not, as did many of those
who perished, flatter Nero or Tigellinus or any other of the
powerful. But he wrote a full account of the Emperor's
deeds of shame, adding the names of his male and female
accomplices and specifying severally their novel forms of
debauchery; and this he sent under seal to Nero. Then he

broke his signet-ring, so that it might not presently serve to endanger others.'

There was grim humour in his presentation to the Emperor. Many victims of Imperial tyranny made rich presents to the tyrant or his minister, so that their kinsfolk or friends might be allowed to inherit the rest.[1] One imagines Nero expectantly opening the parcel— and extracting from it a catalogue of the abominations he had committed. Petronius was a man of bad life, a man infected with that cynical contempt for morality which was characteristic of Nero's court, and yet was not incapable of the lesser kinds of heroism. Galsworthy might well have taken from him a hint for his 'Old English', that unrepentant but gallant old sinner who goes down with colours flying. One might say of Petronius what Talthybius the herald says of Polyxena in Euripides' play:[2] πολλὴν πρόνοιαν εἶχεν εὐσχήμων πεσεῖν, 'much thought he took to fall becomingly': εὐσχήμων, 'like a gentleman'. He was a fit subject for the pencil of Tacitus, the greatest artist in portraiture among all the ancient historians.

A theory that the account of Nero's excesses to which Tacitus refers was no other than the *Satiricon* has found enough support to require mention, but need not delay us long. To write such a work in a few days, at most, and in the circumstances described by Tacitus, would surely have been beyond human powers; and if it had nevertheless been written and sent to Nero as a recognizable lampoon on himself and his court, Nero would certainly have caused it to be destroyed. But in fact there is not in all the novel a character who, viewed as

---

[1] Annaeus Mela, who met his death at the same time as Petronius, is a case in point: cp. Tacitus, *Ann.* xvi. 17. [2] *Hecuba*, 569.

a whole, bears the slightest resemblance to Nero, whereas there are many the delineation of whom bears witness to close observation and study of actual types which could have had no place at an Imperial court. There is no need, however, to labour the argument. It is conceivable, no doubt, that Petronius wrote the *Satiricon* for Nero; but if he did so, he wrote it not for Nero's discomfiture but for his delectation.

I have been calling the novel *Satiricon*, but there is no certainty about the name. Bücheler, the distinguished German editor of Petronius, called it *Satirae*, 'Satires'; improbably, since so obvious a title was not likely to be corrupted into the other recorded names. The name which has gained widest currency in English is *Satyricon*, with a *y*, objectionable because it implies a non-existent connexion with satyrs, and to be regarded as a corrupt spelling of *Satiricon*, the form given (though not on that account necessarily correct) in the oldest manuscript. If *Satiricon* is right, it is a facetiously coined hybrid genitive plural, Latin with a Greek termination, equivalent to *Satiricon libri*, 'books of satirical matters,' i.e. 'Satires'.[1]

Of the text of Petronius' novel we now possess only fragments, presumably detached from the complete work by anthologists. In their sum, they amount, in Bücheler's minor edition, to about a hundred and twenty printed octavo pages. Many of these were known and edited in the fifteenth and sixteenth centuries; but by far the longest and best of them exists in a single manuscript, the famous *Codex Traguriensis*, discovered at Trau in Dalmatia about 1650. It constitutes about a third of what is extant, and contains the episode

---

[1] For this view, see Ernout in the Budé edition of Petronius, p. xxxviii, n. 2.

of the *Cena Trimalchionis*, 'Trimalchio's Dinner', on which the fame of Petronius is most securely based. If some other fragments survive only as witnesses to the depravity of the excerptor, 'Trimalchio's Dinner', at least, owes its preservation to intrinsic merit. With the omission of a very few vulgarities it is fit for the reading of the most modest of youths and maidens. The Trau manuscript[1] states that our excerpts from the *Satiricon* are from the fifteenth and sixteenth books. The statement rests on its sole authority, and is scarcely credible. Even if we assumed that the sixteenth book was also the last, though that is not asserted; further, that the extant fragments represent nearly the whole of Books XV and XVI, though that is neither asserted nor probable; we should still be committed to a work of fiction of a length quite unexampled in antiquity, a work longer than all the sixteen books of Tacitus' *Annals*, longer even than the *Pickwick Papers*.

The standard edition of the Latin text of Petronius is that by Bücheler, and there is a convenient edition of the Latin, with an English translation by Heseltine, in the Loeb Classical Library. I mention also the serviceable edition, with French translation, critical apparatus, and a few explanatory notes, by Ernout in the Budé collection. The episode of Trimalchio's Dinner may be read in a number of separate editions, of which I name only that by W. D. Lowe, with English version and useful commentary. There are also many translations of the whole work, in various languages, without Latin text. Perhaps the most useful of these, for the English reader, is that by J. M. Mitchell in the *Broadway Translations*, though like others it is marred by too free

---

[1] It is now in Paris.

a use of modern colloquialisms where the Latin affords
no warrant for them.

It is not possible to reconstruct the whole story, nor
even, though attempts have been made, to divine, with
any near approach to certainty, its central idea. There
is much in the surviving fragments that is not narrative
at all. For instance, there is much poetry, including an
epyllion, a miniature epic, of nearly three hundred lines
on the Civil War, and a poem of sixty-five lines on the
Sack of Troy; there are also verses which neither are,
nor are intended to be, poetry; there is much literary
criticism: for instance, the famous characterization of
Horace's poetry, *Horatii curiosa felicitas*, 'Horace's elaborate felicity', is thrown off casually by one of Petronius'
characters; and so forth. But let me give a summary.

The action begins in an unnamed town, perhaps
Cumae, not far from Naples, and shifts from time to
time to other parts of southern Italy. The period is the
principate of Nero. The narrator is Encolpius, who is
also the central figure of the story.

In the earlier part of the narrative the principal
characters are two young men named Encolpius and
Ascyltos, and a lad named Giton who is their retainer.
They are precious rogues, all three of them: a set of
well-educated but needy adventurers, always willing
to play the sponger, not averse from a little casual
crime. Their morals are deplorable, and they have no
redeeming virtues. In fact, it would be hard to imagine
a more disreputable gang.

The story, as we now have it, opens abruptly. We
find the two young men engaged in a discussion with
a rhetorician named Agamemnon; or rather, Encolpius

and Agamemnon do the talking while Ascyltos, finding
them tedious, manages to slip away undetected. Encolpius laments the decay of oratory, and criticizes sar-
castically, though justly, the training given by the
schools of rhetoric. Agamemnon admits that his stric-
tures are reasonable, but throws the blame on the
pupils and their parents: in order to earn a living, the
teacher of rhetoric must provide the sort of instruction
that the pupil likes and that the parent at least coun-
tenances; among lunatics, he too must rave.[1] He concludes his reply by setting out his ideas in some im-
promptu verses after the manner of Lucilius. Meanwhile Ascyltos has disappeared. After some alarming
and unsavoury adventures in the back streets of the
town, the two associates manage to find their lodgings,
but presently have a violent quarrel which nevertheless
ends in reconciliation. Here there is a gap in the
narrative.

We next encounter the rogues involved in a little
matter of stolen property. They had purloined some
gold pieces and sewn them into a ragged tunic, which
they had then had the ill luck to lose, leaving themselves with no more than a couple of pence. But they
had also stolen a fine cloak. Coming into a market-
place, they chance upon the rustic owners of the cloak
who have found the lost tunic and are trying to sell it.
Ascyltos makes an opportunity of assuring himself that
the gold pieces are still in it. The friends think of suing
for recovery in the courts, but wisely decide that this
would not be safe. On the other hand, the owners of
the splendid cloak recognize their property. Now en-
sues a pretty piece of wrangling, in the course of which

---

[1] iii. 2 *necesse habent cum insanientibus furere.*

the bystanders propose to impound both garments until a judge can settle the dispute: there is some reason to suspect, as they justly observe, that both articles have been stolen. Ascyltos, however, contrives to procure an exchange, which is apparently to the advantage of the rustics, and the adventurers go off to their inn with the booty.

The next episode is an adventure in which the three are made to suffer for an act of sacrilege. Soon after this, we find them again in the company of the rhetorician Agamemnon, who conducts them to a dinner-party given by the freedman Trimalchio, the description of which, as I have said, takes up about a third of the extant portion of the novel. Of this I postpone consideration.

After the dinner-party there is another quarrel between Encolpius and Ascyltos, and Ascyltos goes off with Giton. Encolpius later recovers Giton, and Ascyltos, having come back in search of the boy, retires discomfited and disappears from the story. In the meantime Encolpius, in depression of spirits, visits a picture-gallery, where he admires works by the old Greek masters. While he thus seeks distraction in the gallery, he meets an old man named Eumolpus, who in the rest of the narrative fills the place left vacant by the withdrawal of Ascyltos.

Eumolpus thus introduces himself: 'I am a poet', he says, 'and a poet, as I hope, not of the meanest inspiration, if only one may put trust in chaplets: though partiality bestows these on the undeserving too. "Why then", you ask, "are your clothes so shabby?" Just for that reason: love of genius never made a man rich.' The two men fall into conversation, and Eumolpus, on this first acquaintance, does not scruple to relate the discreditable particulars of an amorous exploit. Turning to more serious topics, they discuss the decay of art, and Eumolpus, prompted by a picture, composes on the spot, and recites, a poem on the *Sack of Troy*. (In title, but in nothing else, this recalls the poem that Nero is said to have sung, to his own accompaniment, while Rome was burning.)[1] Eumolpus' poem proves that he is indeed a poet of parts, but disapproving hearers throw stones at him till he runs away. Encolpius, though complaining that Eumolpus, during an acquaintance of less than two hours, has spoken more often like a poet than like a human being, takes him to dinner on condition that he indulge his mania no more that day.

Hereafter Encolpius and Eumolpus join forces, and we presently find them, with Giton, on board ship. As happened so often, luck was out. The vessel proves to be the property of a certain Lichas, of Tarentum, who has on board, as passenger, a woman named Tryphaena. These were the very people whom Encolpius and Giton most wished to avoid, since they had been the victims of an earlier escapade. At their wits' end, the rascals try to disguise themselves by shaving their heads and eyebrows, but only make matters worse, because, according to the ancient superstition, to cut the hair on a sea-voyage was to invite disaster. The culprits were thrashed for bringing misfortune on the ship. Worse still, they were recognized, and for a time things threatened to go hardly with them until at last a truce was arrived at. There ensued a terrible storm, in which the ship was wrecked and Lichas was drowned.

[1] Suetonius, *Nero*, 38.

Tryphaena escaped in a boat, and Encolpius and Giton, having been rescued by fishermen, discover Eumolpus in the skipper's cabin spouting poetry with a roar as of a caged beast, and, even in the face of death, filling a huge parchment with his verses. Him, too, they save.

The three friends, safe ashore, find that they are near Crotona, a city notorious for the addiction of its inhabitants to legacy-hunting, one of the popular vices of the time. This happy circumstance suggests to Eumolpus the idea of passing himself off for a wealthy, childless, ailing old man, and thus enriching himself and his two accomplices at the expense of the Crotoniates, who will pay court to him and make gifts. This 'confidence trick' is duly put into execution, and for a time is very profitable. The tricksters live well, if not virtuously, save only that Encolpius is disappointed in a love-affair. But the generosity of the Crotoniates at last begins to flag, and it becomes clear that danger is at hand. Eumolpus therefore announces that his testament will provide only for those, other than his freedmen, who will consent to eat his dead body in public. 'Shut your eyes', he says, 'and imagine that you are eating, not human flesh, but a hundred thousand pounds. And anyhow we'll find some seasonings to change the taste.' And he proceeds to cite allegedly historical precedents for his proposal. The rest of the story is lost.

Observe how very different is all this from the Greek novels. In the *Satiricon* we have no lovely and virtuous heroine, no enamoured and much-enduring hero, no pirates, no rhetorical prinking or posturing or

acrobatics, nothing in fact of the stock-in-trade of your
Tatiuses and Longuses and the rest of them. I grant
the shipwreck, but how differently Petronius manages
it, and with what dramatic effect! Nor can the *Satiricon*
be rightly regarded as a parody of Greek Romance.
Parody by its very nature implies a measure of simi-
larity; but the *Satiricon* differs widely from the Greek
novels in the essentials both of pattern and of substance.
Those who have maintained[1] that Petronius based his
novel, by way either of imitation or of parody, on Greek
original or originals, may be fairly asked, but will be
asked vainly, for trace or record of a possible original.
Where there is demonstrable parody or imitation it is
of Latin, even of contemporary Latin, as in Eumolpus'
poem, after Lucan, on the Civil War. One may doubt
whether these critics have any firmer basis for their
theories than the assumption, too widely current, that
whatever is good in Latin literature must necessarily
have been derived from Greek sources. The *Satiricon*
stands alone, without exemplar and without peer; no
one but a Roman could have written it, and no Roman
but Petronius.

But if I thus claim for Petronius that his work is
unique, I must not be thought to maintain that he
owes nothing to any predecessor. It was the brain of a
a god that gave birth to Pallas, unbegotten and uncon-
ceived. The finite genius of man can do no more than
cultivate the seed that forebears have sown, or engraft
new scions on a stock whose roots are set deep in a past
incalculably remote. To recur to an example of which
I have already made some mention, Quintilian affirms

---

[1] e.g. R. Heinze, 'Petron und der griechische Roman', in *Hermes*, xxxiv
(1899), pp. 494-519.

that Satire is entirely Roman; and if he means that the Romans invented and developed Satire as a separate, well-defined literary species, he speaks truth. And yet Roman satire, before it reached its full development, drew much from the Greeks, without losing its title to essential originality: from drama in the Old Attic Comedy of Aristophanes and the other masters; from the lampoon in Archilochus; from philosophy in the writings of Menippus the Cynic and Bion the Cyrenaic; and so forth: and who shall trace all of these back to their ultimate sources? And so it is with all forms in all literatures. Forgive me for repeating doctrine so well worn as to be trite: Literature is an organism; and though its members are multitudinous and their variety untold, all draw life from a parent stem.

The form of Petronius' novel, a mixture of prose and verse, in which prose greatly predominates, proves his indebtedness to Roman satire of the kind called Menippean, such satire as Varro had written. Perhaps there was a revival of interest in this form in Petronius' day, for to the same period, the Neronian Age, belongs Seneca's Menippean satire the *Apocolocyntosis*, the '*Pumpkinification*' (not Deification) of the Emperor Claudius: a poor thing, in the worst of taste, quite unworthy of its distinguished author. Although it is Menippean in form, Petronius' satire approximates more closely in spirit to that of Horace, taking nothing too seriously, 'telling the truth with a laugh', preferring urbane humour both to ridicule and to moral indignation—for which, indeed, Petronius would have found small warrant in his own character and tastes.

In some details the *Satiricon* is obviously indebted, for manner or matter, or for both, to what were known as the Milesian Tales, although, no less obviously, these cannot have served as model for the whole work. Of the Milesian Tales I have already made passing mention, as one of the factors that contributed to the making of the Greek Romance. They came to be associated with the name of Aristides of Miletus, who collected, and committed to writing, many *novelle* of diverse ages and origins. Some of these were derived from literature, but most, as seems probable, from oral tradition; ordinarily they were both humorous and licentious. You will find many examples of the type in the *Arabian Nights* and the *Decameron*; and there are many more, not recorded in literature, that are still current among people whose taste in fiction is not over-delicate. Aristides' collection of Milesian Tales was translated into Latin in the first half of the first century before Christ by Sisenna—the historian Sisenna, of whom Cicero[1] unkindly said that his pre-eminence among Roman historians merely showed how poor were the achievements of the Romans in this field. Sisenna's version enjoyed great popularity. Plutarch, in his *Life of Crassus*, narrates that when the Romans had been defeated by the Parthians at Carrhae, a copy of Aristides' book (presumably in Sisenna's translation) was found in the pack of a Roman soldier; whereupon the Parthian general spoke contemptuously of Romans as men who even in war could not abstain from obscenities.

The most notable specimen of the Milesian Tale in Petronius is the famous story of the Matron of Ephesus told by the poet Eumolpus on board ship.[2] It is the story of a matron so famed for her wifely virtue that women came from far and near to look upon her. So

---

[1] *Brutus*, 228.   [2] 111 f.

devoted was she to her husband that on his death she
joined him in his underground tomb, determined to
end her life there by starvation. Her parents came, her
kinsfolk, and even the magistrates, but all failed to wean
her from her resolve. Her sole attendant was a faithful
handmaiden, who kept the lamp burning in the tomb.
And there the widow sat, weeping and foodless, for
five days. Then some robbers were crucified, and a
soldier was posted to watch the bodies. Seeing a light
in the tomb, and hearing sounds of lamentation, he
went to investigate. Moved by the woman's grief and
beauty, he tried to comfort her, and offered her his
own food and wine. She refused them, redoubling her
manifestations of grief; but the maid, seduced by the
appetizing odours, made a hearty meal, and at last,
reinforcing her arguments with an apposite quotation,
or rather misquotation, from Virgil,[1]

> Think'st thou that ash or shades of buried dead
> Give heed to this?

persuaded her mistress to do likewise. Thus refreshed,
the widow recovered something of her interest in life,
and presently noticed, for the first time, that the soldier
was a good-looking and well-spoken young fellow. The
soldier, helped by another of the maid's quotations
from Virgil,[2]

> And wilt thou fight against a love approved?

ventured to pay court to her; but while the courtship
proceeded and the soldier was neglecting his duty, the
parents of one of the robbers removed his body from

---

[1] *Aeneid*, iv. 34 *id cinerem aut manes credis curare sepultos?* but the maid substitutes *sentire* for the received text *curare*.

[2] From the same speech of Anna to Dido: *Aen.* iv. 38.

the cross and carried it away. The soldier feared for his life, and therefore, paradoxically, resolved to end it; but the good woman, 'no less pitiful than virtuous', could not bear the loss of a second dear one, and gave him the body of her husband to fix on the cross.

Petronius, then, owed something to the Satire, and something to the Milesian Tale. But there, so far as can be discerned, his specific indebtedness ends. There can be few examples, in any literature, of a work so nearly perfect in its kind that owes so little to predecessors: nothing, in fact, but framework and a few incidentals. Let us consider the *Satiricon* again in relation to the Greek novels. New discoveries, while they afford evidence that there were other kinds of novel, chiefly of quasi-historical content, nevertheless confirm the traditional view, based on the extant examples, that the typical Greek novel was a love-story. In the *Ninus* we have love in combination with what purports to be history. But the *Satiricon*, in any relevant sense, is neither amatory nor historical. In the Greek novels one is accustomed to find, because of their very nature, a heroine as well as a hero, whereas in the *Satiricon* the female characters are subsidiary and incidental. Unless professedly historical, the Greek novels are timeless. Chariton, it is true, makes his heroine the daughter of Hermocrates the Syracusan, a notable historical personage in the fifth century before Christ, and Heliodorus makes his Egypt a Persian satrapy; but these indications of date have no significance for the story, and the other novelists, in this main class, do not even hint, consciously, at a date. The *Satiricon*, on the other hand, while quite certainly not to be classed as an historical

novel, is plainly dated by Petronius in the Neronian
Age, and is therefore a novel of contemporary life and
manners. In the Greek novels that we know, there is
always a contrast and conflict of virtue and villainy,
whereas in the *Satiricon*, while there is some villainy and
plenty of vice, there is no virtue of positive kinds at all.
The chief characters of the Greek novels are persons of
wealth and consideration, those of the *Satiricon* are
totally undistinguished. The Greek novels exhibit
characters who, with few exceptions, are not individuals
but types: in Petronius, every character is clear-cut and
lifelike. This realism in the invention and delineation
of characters is matched by an equal realism in the
scenes. The Greek novelists usually lack the skill, even
if they have the desire, to give the reader a clear impres-
sion of a scene: one may imagine, but does not see,
'what it was like to be there'. But Petronius, with a few
deft touches, gives you the whole scene with an almost
photographic sharpness and particularity: the narrow
winding streets, the footpaths, the market-places, the
inns, the stews with their inscriptions, the baths, the
houses of rich and poor, the fresco-paintings, and all
the rest. All are made vivid and convincing, with
effortless art; and how true they are to reality the remains of Pompeii and Herculaneum bear witness.

All the Greek novelists whose work is extant were professional rhetoricians—'sophist-rhetoricians'—and their
novels are products of their art. This accounts, as we
have seen, for many of their most striking characteristics: their unrealities and absurdities, their irrelevancies
drawn from the common-place book, their artificiality, their passion for display. Rhetoric, they are convinced, can never come amiss, however improbable or

inappropriate the circumstances. Chaereas about to commit suicide;[1] Clitophon contemplating his sweetheart's severed neck;[2] Daphnis watching Chloe asleep;[3] even Habrocomes and Anthea in the bridal chamber;[4] all make speeches that smell, even if they do not positively reek, of the rhetorician's lamp. Hardly less rhetorical is the mould in which the narrative passages are cast. But what of Petronius? Petronius in this matter of rhetoric is a portent. He lived in an age when rhetoric formed the staple of the Roman higher education; a rhetoric, moreover, which, concurrently with the suppression of liberty in public life and in the courts, had become more and more widely divorced from reality. Its marks are almost everywhere on Latin literature of the Silver Age, though the greatest writers avoid its extravagances. In Petronius we encounter the phenomenon of an Imperial writer entirely free from the taint of rhetoric, though himself, no doubt, trained in the customary schools. The schools, on the principle of 'safety first', prescribed to their pupils for declamation or debate themes that had little or no relation to real life. Hear what Petronius, through the mouth of Encolpius, says about them at the opening of the *Satiricon*:

'Isn't it the same kind of Fury that plagues our declaimers? They cry: "For the freedom of the people was I wounded thus!"; "I sacrificed this eye for you!"; "Give me a guide to guide me to my children, for my hamstrings have been cut and cannot support me!". Even this sort of thing would be endurable, if it paved the way to eloquence. But the only issue of this bombast and of this meaningless burble of phrase-making is that the learners, when they come to the bar, think themselves translated into another world. In my

---

[1] Chariton, i. 5.
[2] Achilles Tatius, v. 7.
[3] Longus, i. 25.
[4] Xenophon of Ephesus, i. 9.

opinion, youngsters become absolute numskulls in the schools because they neither hear of nor see anything of our everyday experience: nothing but pirates, with chains, standing on the shore; or tyrants composing edicts that sons shall cut off their fathers' heads; or oracles, given to stop a pestilence, that three or more virgins shall be sacrificed; honey-balls of rhetoric, every word and deed sprinkled with poppy and sesame. Those who are brought up amongst this sort of thing can no more be sound of taste than those who live in a kitchen can be pleasant of smell. With all respect, you rhetoricians have been the first of all to ruin eloquence.'

So Petronius eschews rhetoric, and in this respect also is sharply distinguished from the authors of the Greek romances. In the narrative passages, and the speech of his educated persons, his latinity is as pure and as free from artificialities as you will find in any prose writer after Cicero. But of this more presently.

The *Satiricon* is thoroughly Roman both in matter and spirit, and I ask forbearance if, in emphasizing this, I draw attention again to some points on which I have touched already. We have seen how the generalizing Greek genius tends to exhibit the type rather than the individual, in literature as well as in other forms of art; and in so far as Rome is under the influence of Greece, the same tendency persists, as may be observed notably in Latin Comedy. But the Roman is by nature a realist, interested in the particular rather than in the general. It was not by accident that in sculpture, for instance, the Romans achieved their best work in historical sculptures and in portraits, as is proved by countless surviving examples. In the *Satiricon* there are many types: the millionaire freedman, the teacher of rhetoric, the poet-adventurer, the patchwork-blanket maker, the monumental mason, the quarrelsome wife, and so forth; but each of these is strongly individualized and each is drawn with a vivid realism that has not been surpassed even in the modern novel: in the ancient literatures there is nothing to approach it. Miraculous skill in the delineation of character is among the greatest of Petronius' virtues as a novelist: no matter how insignificant the character may be, however small a part he may play, there he stands before us, individual and complete and alive. What mere marionettes, in comparison, are most of the characters of the Greek novels!

The characters of Petronius are all of types familiar in the Rome and Italy of his day, accurately observed and sketched with a humour which gives to him a very high place among the humorists of the world. How thoroughly he enjoyed writing his book! Latin literature as a whole, like the Peers in *Iolanthe*, is 'dignified and stately'. It is written for men of station, and is apt to shut out from its august consideration men of lowlier degree—the slave, the freedman, the tradesman, the artisan. From literature we learn little about the common folk of Rome and Italy. But all of Petronius' characters are taken from the humbler walks of life. They include the rich with the poor, the educated with the ignorant; but one and all are, as I have said, altogether undistinguished. This indolent courtier, this able and energetic statesman—for he was both—this cultured voluptuary, took a most comprehensive interest in humanity; and it amused him to record the lives and idiosyncrasies and conversation of men and women whom the average Roman noble would regard either not at all or with indulgent contempt. That most of his characters bear Greek names is due not to derivation

from some Greek source, but primarily, one may suppose, to the fact that the scenes of the story are laid in
southern Italy,[1] a land thickly studded with towns of
Greek origin, the towns of what was once called 'Great
Greece'. This at any rate makes the use of Greek names
appropriate. But it is also possible, I think, that Petronius preferred the thin disguise of foreign names when
indicating, as he often does, by his choice of name some
characteristic or occupation of the bearer. Of this device, of course, though it is now out of fashion, even
modern literature has furnished many examples, and
Petronius makes free, though not invariable, use of it.[2]
Thus Encolpius suggests 'Cuddle'; Ascyltos 'Thick-
skin'; Giton 'Neighbour'; Eumolpus 'Sweetsong'. The
chief rhetorician is called Agamemnon, 'King of men',
and his second-in-command is therefore named Menelaus. Tryphaena is voluptuous, as her name denotes;
Circe is as amorous as Homer's enchantress; Pannychis
is 'Miss Nightrevel'. Trimalchio, the fabulously
wealthy freedman, has a hybrid name, half Greek and
half Semitic, which has been interpreted 'Thrice
Blessed'.

Petronius is no less complete a realist in language
than in character-drawing. Latin falls into three main
divisions, all of which are abundantly represented in
Petronius. In narrative passages he uses literary Latin

[1] A couple of fragments, preserved by other writers, point to the possibility,
though not the certainty, that the scene of a lost part of the novel was Massilia
(the modern Marseilles), an ancient Greek foundation in which Greek names
would be equally appropriate.

[2] It is perhaps relevant to observe that in Latin fiction a Greek name does
not necessarily imply Greek nationality or derivation or even habits. In
Martial's Epigrams, for instance, there is nothing un-Roman about a Chaere-
stratus who for lack of a few pounds loses his right to a place on the Knights'
benches in the theatre (Mart. Epigr. v. 25).

which, though less formal than the Latin of the more
dignified masters, is of such excellence that because of
it the Council of Trent refrained from putting the
Satiricon on the Index. His educated characters, such
as Encolpius and Eumolpus, speak what was known as
sermo urbanus or *sermo cotidianus*, the everyday Latin of
educated Romans, the Latin best exemplified in the
correspondence of Cicero and his friends. But the humbler, uneducated persons, such as Trimalchio and his
associates, speak the *sermo plebeius*, for which indeed
Petronius is one of our chief authorities. This was the
speech of the common people, 'Vulgar Latin' as it is
sometimes called, the sort of Latin from which the
Romance languages—Italian, French, Spanish, and
the rest—are in the main descended. In Petronius we
find a Campanian variety of Vulgar Latin, in which
there is a considerable admixture of Greek words; just
the sort of Latin, except that in Petronius there are few
vagaries of spelling to indicate popular pronunciations,
that is to be read in the multitude of inscriptions scrib-
bled, in the same era, on walls in the Campanian towns
of Pompeii and Herculaneum, and now recorded in
volume IV of the great Corpus of Latin Inscriptions.
In vocabulary and accidence and syntax it differs very
greatly even from the everyday colloquial speech of the
educated, and still more from literary Latin; it abounds
in hybrids and slang and irregular formations that
would horrify a purist, and exhibits a delightful
uncertainty in the use of genders and declensions
and conjugations; but withal it is vigorous, forth-
right, and racy, admirably adapted to the expression
of simple ideas, and, in Petronius' use of it, contri-
butes, hardly less than the thoughts of which it is the

vehicle, to our comprehension and realization of character. Petronius' astonishing skill in adapting speech to character will become apparent, I hope, when I come, as I shall do now, to the episode of Trimalchio's Dinner.

Trimalchio's Dinner is a study of a vulgar multi-millionaire and his friends, a good-humoured satire on the freedmen *nouveaux riches* of whom there were so many in Imperial Rome. Agamemnon, the professor of rhetoric, has himself been bidden to the dinner-party, and has obtained invitations for Encolpius, Ascyltos, and Giton. These three forget all their troubles, put on their best clothes, and go off to the baths. At the baths, says Encolpius, 'all at once we see a bald-headed old man dressed in a red tunic and playing ball among long-haired pages. It was not so much the pages that had made us look, though they were worth looking at, as his lordship himself, who was wearing dress-shoes and taking exercise with a green ball. He wouldn't pick up a ball that had touched the ground, but a slave had a bag full of them, from which he kept supplying the players.' This was Trimalchio, their host. After exercise and the bath, he donned a scarlet wrap, entered his palanquin, and moved off homeward preceded by four liveried footmen and a go-cart containing his blear-eyed wizened favourite, 'uglier than Trimalchio himself'.

Following their host, the friends presently reach the house. Here again they encounter the ostentation of gay colours, costly as well as abnormal, and therefore a favourite extravagance of Trimalchio and his household. At the door there was a janitor dressed in green with a cherry-coloured girdle, shelling peas in a silver dish; and above, in a golden cage, a magpie was squawking a how-do-you-do to the guests as they came in. This was only a foretaste of the splendours of the house. They pass through a long colonnade decorated, in fresco-painting, with scenes from the life of Trimalchio, and enter a vast hall, the *atrium* of the mansion, in which the pictures are of scenes from the *Iliad* and the *Odyssey* and a recent gladiatorial show. And so they reach the dining-hall. Here everything was done to music: if a slave rendered a service, he sang; if he was asked for something, he sang; and the singing was very bad. In fact, it was more like a vaudeville show than a gentleman's dining-room.

With excellent dramatic effect, Petronius delays Trimalchio's entrance till after the *hors-d'œuvres*. At last Trimalchio, his shaven head protruding from a voluminous scarlet cloak, a fringed and purple-bordered table-napkin about his neck, a silver toothpick in action, is carried in to the music of a band and set down on the couch in the midst of a pile of tiny cushions. 'My friends', he says, with exquisite courtesy, 'I didn't want to come to dinner yet, but rather than keep you waiting by my absence I have quite forgone my own pleasure. Still, you'll let me finish my game of chess first.' And this he does, swearing the while 'like a mill-hand'.

Trimalchio does his guests extremely well, in wine as well as food. 'Wine', he says, 'is life. This is real Opimian. What I served yesterday wasn't as good, and my guests were much finer gentlemen.' But he must not only be lavish, he must also be original; and his idea of originality is to serve a series of 'freak' dishes

such as we used to be told would be provided on great
occasions by the baser sort of modern American millionaire. It is all very ingenious, all very costly, and all
most marvellously vulgar. A wooden hen, brooding on
peahen's eggs in a basket of straw, is brought in to the
accompaniment of music. The eggs are handed round,
and Trimalchio expresses the fear that they are addled;
but they prove to contain dainty figpeckers in a paste
of flour and devilled yolk-of-egg. There was a great
circular tray on which were represented the signs of the
Zodiac, and on each sign was an appropriate dish: beef
on the Bull, mullet on the Fish, kidneys on the Twins,
and so on. A wild boar, the most highly prized of all
ancient game, was carried in: a gigantic bearded slave,
garbed as a huntsman, ripped it up with a hunting-
knife, and out flew, not 'four-and-twenty blackbirds',
but a flock of thrushes, one of which was given to each
guest.

All the dinner is of a piece with that. And the ser-
vants are in keeping. We meet a cook who can make
anything out of anything: goose and fish and game-
fowl out of plain pig, fish out of a sow's matrix, pigeon
out of fat bacon, squab out of ham; Trimalchio, with
pretty wit, as he says, has dubbed him Daedalus. There
is the carver happily named Carpus, whence one of
Trimalchio's standing jokes: when a dish is brought in,
Trimalchio cries 'Carpe, carpe!' that is 'Carver, carve
'er!' And there is the well-meaning young slave who
insults the master by picking up a silver dish that he
has dropped, instead of letting it be swept out with the
debris of the meal.

The company does not spend all the time in eating
and drinking. There is plenty of talk, and plenty of

entertainment. Trimalchio, who is no dull-witted igno-
ramus—a man needs education these days, even at
dinner; and his patron, bless him, saw to it that he was
made a man among men—Trimalchio bids a guest tell
of the twelve labours of Hercules, and how the Cyclops
screwed Ulysses' thumb out, tales that he used to read
in Homer when a boy. And he knows how Hannibal
invented Corinthian bronze at the sack of Troy, how
Ajax went mad because Iphigenia married Achilles,
how Niobe was shut up in the Trojan Horse by Daedalus. It is excellent fooling. A guest tells a gruesome
tale of a werewolf, the first werewolf story in literature,
which Trimalchio caps with a still more horrifying tale
of witches. A secretary reads out his report, 'as though
it were the City Gazette':[1]

'*July 26th*: On the estate at Cumae, property of Trimalchio, born 30 boys, 40 girls; transferred from threshing-
floor to granary, 500,000 pecks of grain; oxen broken in, 500.

Same date: The slave Mithridates was crucified for cursing
our master Gaius; put away in the safe, because it could not
be invested, £100,000.

Same date: A fire, originating in the overseer Nasta's house,
occurred in the gardens at Pompeii.[2]

On hearing this last entry recited, Trimalchio exclaims
'What's that? When were the gardens at Pompeii
bought for me?' 'Last year,' replies the secretary, 'and
so they haven't come on the books yet.' Trimalchio
flared up and said, 'If properties are bought for me and

---

[1] 53, 1 ff. The *Urbis acta* were the *acta diurna* ('Daily News'), the official daily
gazette of Rome.
[2] This, I have no doubt, is the meaning of *in hortis Pompeianis*, not, as Ernout
(Indices, p. 210) strangely takes it, 'in the gardens belonging to Pompeius',
i.e. to (Pompeius) Trimalchio. A local name is needed, as in *praedio Cumano*,
just above; and Trimalchio's estates extend not only to Pompeii but far beyond.

I don't know within six months, I won't 'ave them
entered on my books.'

Trimalchio grows maudlin and causes his will to be
read, so that he may be loved as much in life as in death.
All the beneficiaries are touched by his generosity. He
then reduces himself and the company to tears by giving
directions for his funeral. Here are some of them, addressed to his friend the monumental mason Habinnas,
who will have the contract for making the tomb.[1]

Turning to Habinnas, he said: 'What about it, dear old
friend? Are you building my monument as I told you to?
I'm mighty anxious to have you paint by the feet of my
statue a pup, and wreaths of flowers, and perfumes, and all
Petraites's[2] fights, so that thanks to you I may enjoy life
when I'm dead. Make the frontage a hundred feet, the
depth two-hundred: I want all sorts of fruit about my ashes,
and lots of vines. It's plain wrong to have a man's houses
nice when he's alive and not to bother about those where
we have to be longer. And that is why above all I want put
on it "'This monument is not to descend to the heir"'.

'Yes, and I'll see to it that I provide in my will for not
being insulted when I am dead. I am going to put one of
my freedmen in charge of my tomb to guard it, so that folk
mayn't make a dash to my monument to do their business.
And please do ships[3] under full sail (on the wall) of my
monument, and me sitting on a platform in official robes
with five gold rings and pouring out cash to a crowd out of
a bag; for you know, I gave a banquet at two shillings a
head. I'd like the dinin'-'all to be did too. And you'll do
the whole people doing themselves well. On my right you'll

---

[1] Chapter 71.
[2] An eminent gladiator. Trimalchio (ch. 52) already has a number of cups
decorated with his exploits in the arena.
[3] These are to symbolize Trimalchio's trading ventures by sea.

put a statue of my dear Fortunata[1] with a dove in her hand:
and have her with her pup on a lead tied to her belt; and
put my kid[2], and some large jars sealed so as not to let the
wine spill. And you may carve a broken urn and a boy
crying over it. A sundial in the middle, so that whoever
looks at the time reads my name willy nilly. And the
inscription—think carefully—how will this do? "C. Pompeius Trimalchio Maecenatianus[3] rests here. He was appointed an Augustal[4] in his absence. He could have been on
every civil service panel at Rome, but refused. Dutiful,
brave, and loyal, he grew from small beginnings and left
thirty millions of sesterces. And he never went to a lecture.
Farewell: and thou also." '

After this lugubrious performance all are dissolved in
tears, even Encolpius the narrator. At the suggestion
of Trimalchio, they all troop out and take a hot bath,
during which Encolpius and his friends try to escape.
Unsuccessful in their attempt, they return with the rest
to renew the festivity. At last Trimalchio ordered horn-
blowers to be fetched into the dining-room and to 'play
something pretty' while he pretended to be dead. The
band struck up a dirge. One of the bandsmen, the son
of an undertaker, outblew the others and produced
such a thunderous din that the whole neighbourhood
was aroused, and the fire brigade, thinking that the
house was afire, smashed in the door and set to work

[1] His wife, with whom we shall find him quarrelling violently.

[2] *Cicaronem meum*: presumably the favourite, mentioned above.

[3] This imposing array of names, assumed by Trimalchio on receiving his
freedom, does no more than suggest the eminence, wealth, and munificence
of Trimalchio's former masters. Chronology, propriety, and the context alike
forbid us to suppose that Petronius represents his Trimalchio as a quasi-
historical character, formerly the slave of Maecenas and, after him, of a
Pompeius.

[4] The *Augustales*, six in number, held a sort of honorary magistracy. In the
towns of southern Italy they were always freedmen.

with water and axes. In the confusion the friends at last made their escape.

Here is Fortunata, the appropriately named wife of Trimalchio, as described to Encolpius, in chapter 37, by his neighbour at table:

'That's Trimalchio's wife: Fortunata is her name; she measures her cash by the peck. And only the other day, what was she? You'll excuse me, sir, you wouldn't have taken bread from her hand. Now, without why or wherefore, she's God almighty and Trimalchio's factotus. In fact, if it's mid midday and she tells him it's dark, he'll believe her. He doesn't know what he has: he's fairly rolling in it; but this bitch[1] sees to everything, and where you wouldn't expect it. She's a steady, sensible body, full of good ideas: why, look at all this gold! But she has a nasty tongue, and clacks and clacks in bed. If she likes you she likes you, if she doesn't she doesn't.'

And having introduced her, Petronius leaves her to reveal herself, for the rest, by word and action.

I have tried in this translation, and elsewhere, to give you something of the flavour of the Latin, a task not easy to accomplish. So much turns, in the speech of Petronius' humbler characters, on the use of a vulgar word or inflexion or turn of phrase for which it is hard to find a satisfactory analogue in English. One can only do one's best, avoiding the excesses of colloquialism and vulgarism, not justified by the Latin, that mar some of the current versions. Some of these humble

---

[1] This, it seems, is the meaning of *lupatria*. If I understand it aright, the name is not a reflection on Fortunata's morals, which, in the context, are not impugned. On vulgar lips a coarse word may merely express some strong emotion, as, in this instance, of admiration. Similarly in English one may hear a word which, if taken literally, would be a foul insult, used as an expression of affection and sympathy by those who lack both refinement and an adequate vocabulary.

folk at Trimalchio's party know very well that their
speech is vulgar and ungrammatical, and are sensitive
about it. Here again Petronius' psychology is exactly
right. Thus Echion the blanket-maker,[1] after a long
discourse, notices that the rhetorician Agamemnon is
smiling at his blunders, and forthwith, in his indignation, blunders worse: 'I can see you're saying, Agamemnon, "Why is that nuisance babbling?" Because
you, who *can* gab, won't gab. You're not one of our
bunch, and so make fun of the way us *poor* coves talk.
We know *you* are silly with edication.'

Here is Seleucus,[2] fresh from a funeral, speaking
after another guest has mentioned baths and wine.
The type is not yet extinct:

'I don't take a bath every day. A bath is like the laundryman:[3] the water has teeth. Every day, and our innards
melt. But when I've got inside a mug of mead,[4] to hell with
the cold. Anyhow I couldn't have had a bath, for I was to
a funeral to-day. Chrysanthus—a nice, decent chap he was
—has snuffed out. It was only the other day he spoke to me.
It seems as if I was talking with him now. Dear, oh dear!
We are just blown bags on legs. We're of less account than
flies. Flies have *some* good in them, anyhow; but we are of
no more account than bubbles. And suppose he hadn't
starved himself. For five days he didn't chuck water into his
mouth, and not a speck of bread. And yet he's joined the

---

[1] Ch. 46. Echion is a *centonarius*, a maker of the rag blankets which, soaked
in water, were used for putting out fires.

[2] Ch. 42.

[3] Literally 'fuller'. The *fullo* was the bleacher and laundryman and 'cleaner'
of the Roman world, here the butt of the ancient jest that we now direct at
the laundryman.

[4] Mead is an excellent substitute for a cloak. Cp. *Gammer Gurton's Needle*:
'No frost nor snow, no wind, I trow, | Can hurt me if it wold: | I am so
wrapped within and lapped | Of jolly good ale and old.'

majority.[1] 'Twas the doctors did for him, or rather his bad 'oroscope; for a doctor is nothing but a comfort to the mind. Still, he had a lovely funeral, with a proper bier and a lovely pall. The mourning was very fine (he set some of his people free), even if his wife was stingy with her tears. Suppose he hadn't treated her well. But your woman who *is* a woman is a regular kite. Nobody oughtn't to do none of them a kindness: it's just like chucking it into a well. But an old love sticks like a crab.'

And next let us listen to Ganymedes the pessimist:[2]

'What he's telling us is neither here nor there. But nobody minds how prices is pinching. Good God! I haven't been able to find a mouthful of bread today. And how the drought lasts! We've been starving for a year now. Blast the Flour Board.[3] They're up to their games with the millers: "you scratch my back, I'll scratch yours". And so the small man is in trouble; for with those big bugs it's always Christmas. Oh, if only we had those stout fellers I found here when I first came from Asia! A man could live then. . . . The way they used to wallop those stiffs and put the fear of God into them! Yes, and I remember Safinius. He lived up by the old arch in those days, when I was a lad. A perfect peppercorn: hot!—wherever he went he singed the ground. But he was straight, he was sure, a friend to a friend, a man you wouldn't mind playing odd-and-even with in the dark. . . . A penny loaf was more than enough for two; but now I've seen a bull's eye bun bigger. Dear, oh dear! it's getting worse every day. This colony is growing backwards like a calf's tail.'

In the speech of all the uneducated persons there is a vulgar element, but this element varies in amount and kind with the individual. Petronius is too close an

---

[1] Seleucus does use this *cliché*, *abiit ad plures*, much as Niceros (below) says *supremum diem obiit* 'breathed his last'. [2] Ch. 44.

[3] The *aediles*, whose duties included superintendence of markets and food supplies.

observer and too true an artist to make all speak alike, and he differentiates one character from another not only in what is said but also in the manner of saying it. To illustrate satisfactorily, in translations, this aspect of Petronius' realism would be extremely difficult if not actually impossible, and I venture only on a single example. Niceros, who tells the story of the werewolf,[1] makes a specialty of the 'bulls' that we call Irish. Admonished by Trimalchio not to be so glum, he says he is afraid that those scholar fellows will laugh at him; but plucking up courage he adds: 'Well, that 's their business. I'll tell it all the same. Let them laugh: it doesn't hurt me. It 's better to be laughed at than made ridiculous.' And so he begins his tale:

'When I was still in service, we were living in Narrow Street: Gavilla has the house now.' (Note how these details give an air of reality to the narrative as when we are told that Safinius 'used to live by the old arch'.) 'There, as the gods willed, I fell in love with the wife of Terence who used to keep the pub; you knew her: Melissa from Tarentum, the prettiest peach of a woman. But so help me, it was not for her looks or for what I could get that I went with her, but because she was a good honest lass. If I asked her for anything, she never said no. If she made a penny, I had a ha'penny; (all that I had) I gave her to mind, and I was never took down. Her man breathed his last out at the homestead. And so, by tooth and toe-nail, I made and managed a way to come to her. You know, it 's trouble that shows the friend.

'It happened that the master was put to Capua to fix up some odds and ends. Taking my chance, I persuaded of a guest of ours to come with me as far as the fifth milestone. A soldier he was, strong as the devil. We vamoose about

---

[1] Chapters 61 and 62.

cockcrow; the moon was as bright as at midday. We come among the tombs: my man goes to do his job by the pillars, and I sit there singing and counting the pillars. Then, when I looked back for my mate, he undressed himself and put all his clothes by the roadside. My heart was in my mouth, and I stood like I was dead. But he made a ring of water round his clothes, and suddenly turned into a wolf. Don't think I am joking: I wouldn't tell a lie, not for anybody's fortune. But as I was going to say, when he turned into a wolf he began to howl and ran off into the wood. At first I didn't know where I was; then I went to pick up his clothes, but they were turned into stone. Didn't I just die of fear! Still, I drew my sword, and whackity-whack!,[1] I cut at the shadows until I came to the homestead of my lady friend. I came in like a corpse; I nearly snuffed out; the sweat fairly flew between my legs; my eyes went dead; I hardly came to at all. My lass Melissa wondered why I was out walking so late, and says she: "If you had come sooner, you would at least have helped us. A wolf came into the homestead; and all the cattle, he let 'em blood like a butcher. But he didn't have the laugh of us, even if he did get away: one of our people ran him through with a spear." When I heard this, I could not sleep another wink; but when it was broad day I ran for my master Gaius' house like a robbed publican, and when I came to the place where the clothes had been turned into stone I found nothing but blood. And when I got home, my soldier was lying in bed like a bullick and the doctor was seeing to his neck. I knew then that he was a change-skin, and after that I couldn't have taken a bite of bread with him, not if you had killed me first.'

But in observing the guests, perhaps we have been

---

[1] The manuscript gives *matauitatau*, which has been variously emended. May it not be, after all, as one of the seventeenth century editors suggested, an onomatopoeic coinage? I should put stresses on the second and last syllables. Note that the incongruity of a sword noisily *whacking* unsubstantial shadows is quite in the manner of the speaker.

too neglectful of the host. Before we leave the dinner, let us hear what Trimalchio has to say for himself. By this time all the company are a little the worse for liquor, and Trimalchio so far forgets himself as to kiss a pretty servant. His wife Fortunata is furious; she swears at him and calls him 'riff-raff' and 'disgrace' and, finally, 'dog'. Trimalchio throws a cup at her and hits her on the cheek. There are tears on the one side and vilification on the other: Trimalchio won't have her statue on his tomb, for even then she would give him no peace. He won't even let her kiss him when he's dead. Habinnas, who is to make the tomb, and his wife Scintilla both beg him to relent, until Trimalchio, bursting into tears, speaks as follows:[1]

'Habinnas, sure as I 'ope you may enjoy your pile, if I did wrong, spit in my face. I kissed a thoroughly good girl, not because she's pretty but because she's good. She knows her ten-times, she can read a book at sight, she has made herself a fancy-dress out of her allowance and bought a chair and two ladles out of her own money. Doesn't she deserve to have me take notice of her? But Fortunata says no. You would, would you, Madame high-heels? Take my advice: don't let your luck give you the stomach-ache, you kite; don't make me show my teeth, sweetie, or you'll feel my dander. You know me: when I once make up my mind there's no budging me. But let us remember the living. Please enjoy yourselves, friends. You know, I was once just like you: it was merit that brought me to this. It's the little brain that makes men, everything else is plain rubbidge. "I buy well, I sell well"; though others will tell you differently. I am bursting with success. What, snuffler? Still crying? I'll soon make you cry, for what's coming to you. Well, as I was going to say, it was levelheadedness that

[1] Chapters 75 to 77. I make one small change *pudoris causa*.

brought me to this fortune. When I came from Asia, I was just so high as this candelabrus is. In fact, every day I used to measure myself by it. And so as to get a moustache under my beak quicker, I used to rub oil from the lamps on my lips. For fourteen years I was the boss's favourite: there's nothing wrong in what the boss tells you to do. And I pleased the missus too. You know what I mean. I say nothing: I'm not one to boast.

'Well, by the grace of God, I ran the house and, look you, took the boss's fancy. In short, he made me co-heir with the Emperor, and I got a nobleman's fortune. But nobody's never satisfied. I must needs try trading. To cut it short, I built five ships, I loaded wine—it was just gold in those days—, I sent them to Rome. You'd think I'd ordered it: all the ships were wrecked. It 's not a story, it 's the truth. In one day Neptune swallowed three hundred thousand pounds. Think I lost heart? No! Why, I thought this loss nobbut a mouthful, practically nothing. I built a second lot, bigger and better and luckier, so that everybody was saying I was a stout fellow. You know, a great ship is a stout ship. I loaded up again, with wine and fat bacon and beans and scent and slaves. This time Fortunata did the decent thing: she sold all her gold and all her clothes and put a hundred sovereigns into my hand. That was the yeast that made my pile rise. Things go so fast when the gods will. On a single trip I cleared a round hundred thousand pounds. At once I bought back all the properties that had belonged to my patron. I build a house, I buy up slaves and cattle; everything I touched grew like a honeycomb. When I found that I had more than all my home-town together, 'twas "hand from the board!".[1] I got clear of trading and began financing freedmen. But when I wanted to retire from my business, an astrologer wouldn't 'ave it. This was a Greek bloke, name of Serapa, who had happened to come to our

---

[1] i.e. 'the game is over'.

colony:[1] he was in the know with the gods. He even told me what I had forgotten, explained everything to me from A to Z. He knew me inside out: could almost tell me what I had had for dinner yesterday. You'd have thought he had always lived with me. I ask you, Habinnas—you were there, I think—: "That 's how you came by your missus"; "You are not very lucky in your friends"; "No one ever makes you a fair return"; "You have great estates"; "You are nursing a viper in your bosom"; and—I touch wood[2]— that I still have left to live thirty years and four months and two days. And besides, I'm soon to receive a legacy. This my 'oroscope tells me. If I manage to join my estates up with Apulia,[3] I'll have come far enough in life. In the meantime, under Mercury's eye, I have built this house. As you know, it was a bit of a shanty: now it's a palace. It has four dining-rooms, twenty private rooms, two marble colonnades; upstairs, a lot of small rooms, my own bedroom, this viper's lair, a first-rate crib for the janitor. There's plenty of room for guests. In fact, when Scaurus came here, there was nowhere he preferred to stay, and he has friends of his father to stay with at the seaside. And there is plenty else that I'll show you presently. Believe me, have a penny, and you're worth a penny; have something, and you'll be thought something. So your friend, who was once a frog, is now a king.'

Trimalchio then orders in his funeral robes for the inspection of his guests; the bandsmen are brought in to play a dirge; the fire-brigade arrives; and so the party breaks up in confusion.

What direct influence, if any, the *Satiricon* has had on modern literature I shall not attempt to estimate. It

[1] The 'colony', of course, is a town with 'colonial' status.

[2] Literally, 'why shouldn't I tell you?' Like his fellows, Trimalchio is superstitious; but he decides, being emboldened with wine, to take the risk.

[3] A modest hope. Trimalchio will be content, say, with no more than a third of Italy.

is the first picaresque novel, and on that account, if on no other, would demand attention. All of it is heartless, and the grossness of parts is extreme. But in humour, and in brilliance of conception and execution, it is a masterpiece; and the loss of the Trimalchio episode, so narrowly averted, would have caused a lamentable impoverishment of the world's literature.

THE GOLDEN ASS

IN the *Golden Ass*, the last of the novels to be considered, we have a specimen of a different genre. In it
we shall see what a young Roman provincial of genius,
temporarily resident at Rome, and writing in Latin,
was able to make of a tale the outline of which he found
ready to his hand in Greek. I have told the worst: Apuleius borrowed—an ancient would not have said 'stole'
—the essentials of his plot. And yet he developed
from these a novel to which it would be absurd to deny
the merit of originality, a novel which may be justly regarded as the greatest achievement of the ancients in
prose fiction, with the sole possible exception of the
Satiricon. In so far as it is of Greek derivation, the
Golden Ass represents for us a kind of Greek novel that
bears little resemblance to the *erotica*, the love-stories,
of Achilles Tatius and the rest. The main narrative
relates the adventures of a man who, dabbling un-
wisely in magic, was changed into an ass. But Apuleius
gives us very full measure. He interposes in his story
many examples of the *novella*, which in due course were
to furnish models and material for Boccaccio and other
Italian *novellieri*, who in turn transmitted the influence
to England and other countries. And he includes, as
a romance within a romance, the delightful tale of
Cupid and Psyche, which has left its mark on English
literature from the *Faerie Queene* of Spenser to the *Eros
and Psyche* of Bridges.

Apuleius, the author of the *Golden Ass*, was a native of
Madaura, an important town of North Africa in the

part now called Algeria. The date of his birth is not known exactly, but may be set at about A.D. 125, so that his lifetime falls mainly within the age of the Antonines. His first name is commonly given as Lucius, but only on the authority of late manuscripts which may derive it from the identification of Apuleius with his hero Lucius in the last book of the *Golden Ass*. His father attained the highest public office in Madaura, that of *duumvir*, corresponding to the consulship in Rome, and gave to his son an education befitting his exalted station. After attending an elementary school at Madaura, the young Apuleius was sent to Carthage, where he continued his studies in the schools of the grammarian and the rhetorician.

As a rule, the formal education of the wealthy young Roman or provincial went no farther. Apuleius, however, proceeded from Carthage to Athens, which was still the chief seat of learning in the Empire, providing for the whole Gracco-Roman world the equivalent of a university. There he pursued a great variety of studies: poetics, geometry, music, dialectic, philosophy in all its branches. He seems to have made Athens his head-quarters from the eighteenth to about the twenty-fourth year of his age; but being an unattached student, he managed also during these years to travel extensively, enlarging his knowledge not only of mundane things but also of the religions of the countries that he visited. He caused himself to be initiated into certain mystery-religions, among them that of the Egyptian Isis. With what fervour of devotion she inspired him appears plainly in the last book of the *Golden Ass*.

Apuleius, by the standards of his time, was a very wealthy young man, for his father had bequeathed to him a fortune of about ten thousand pounds. But he left Athens comparatively poor, though still far from beggary. He had spent much of his money, not only on his studies and travels, but also in subsidies to needy acquaintances and liberal gifts to his teachers, and even in providing dowries for the daughters of friends. In recording this,[1] the excellent fellow says that there are some acts of decency and generosity which would be worth the sacrifice of a whole patrimony.

At the age of about twenty-five Apuleius came to Rome. There he settled for a time, learning, as he says, with painful effort and without a teacher, to speak Latin as the Romans themselves spoke it, and earning a livelihood by practice at the bar. It is very probable, if not quite certain, that while he was thus engaged at Rome he wrote and published the *Metamorphoses*, the name by which he himself called the *Golden Ass*, an extraordinarily brilliant achievement for so young a man. He was probably not quite thirty when he left Rome for his home in Africa. Almost at once, as seems likely, he set out on his travels again, intending to visit Alexandria; but on his way along the coast to Alexandria he fell ill and broke his journey at Oea, near the modern Tripoli. There he married a rich widow, about ten years older than himself, whose name was Aemilia Pudentilla.

It was the elder Mr. Weller (was it not?) who counselled the avoidance of widows. Apuleius lived seventeen centuries too soon to profit by the warning. The lady's relations so resented the marriage that they brought him to trial for the practice of magic, alleging that he had used magical means to win for himself

[1] *Apologia*, 23.

a wealthy wife. Apuleius defended himself in an extant speech, the *De Magia* or *Apologia*, which is the chief source of what we know about his life. His defence was as follows.

On his way to Alexandria, Apuleius made a halt at Oea, where he was visited by Pontianus, the son of Aemilia Pudentilla, whom he had known and helped when they were students together at Athens. Pontianus, who was by some years the younger, urged him to become his mother's guest. This ingenuous young man, having learnt that his mother, after a long widowhood, had decided, on the advice of her doctors, to marry again, had hurried from Rome to Oea so that he might have a finger in this unexpected matrimonial pie. When his old friend Apuleius arrived, Pontianus discovered in him an altogether desirable stepfather, and told him so. Pudentilla 'was willing'. Apuleius, on the other hand, was wary; but on becoming better acquainted, he agreed. Meanwhile Pontianus himself had married the daughter of one Herennius Rufinus. Egged on by his father-in-law, he now changed front and tried to prevent the match; but later, he became reconciled. Apuleius married Pudentilla, and has left on record his appreciation of her wifely virtues. Sidonius Apollinaris, in the fifth century, names her among a number of exemplary women who would help their husbands in their studies by holding candles for them.[1]

Within a year or so of the marriage, Pontianus died. His younger brother Pudens was then persuaded by Herennius to prosecute Apuleius, charging him with having bewitched Pudentilla. The accusers even alleged that Apuleius had murdered Pontianus, though

[1] Sid. Apoll. *Epist.* ii. 10.

they did not charge him with this formally. The case was tried before the governor of the province, Claudius Maximus, and Apuleius was acquitted. Of his career thereafter we have no connected account. It is known, however, that he lived for a time at Carthage, where he was elected to the highest office tenable by a provincial, that of *sacerdos provinciae*, high-priest of the province. His eminence as an orator won him many distinctions, such as statues and honorific decrees, in various towns that he visited. The date of his death is unknown.

Apuleius was one of Fortune's favourites. To wealth and a handsome person he added the best schooling that Africa afforded, years of further study at Athens, much travel in many lands; these, used with a keen intelligence, enriched him with an experience of the world and an encyclopaedic knowledge such as few men of his time can have possessed. Taking all knowledge for his province, he was immensely proud of his versatility. He was master of Greek as well as of Latin, and published works in both languages. He was a finished writer of verse, no less than of prose. By profession, like so many of the ancient novelists, he was a sophist-rhetorician, practising his art both in the lawcourts and on public platforms, but practising it as a man of the world with a strong grip on reality. He was also a copious writer on philosophical subjects, earning for himself, notably, the title of *Platonicus*; he dabbled in natural science; he composed histories; he seems to have written at least one other novel besides the *Metamorphoses*.

It is only with the last of all these works, however, that we are now concerned. The more familiar title of the *Metamorphoses, Asinus Aureus, The Golden Ass,* is witness to the admiration of a Father of the Church: it appears first in the *De Civitate Dei* of the African St. Augustine, who died in the year 430. The epithet *aureus,* 'golden', indicates at once the superiority of this very human and intelligent ass to asses of the common sort, and the golden quality of a most delightful romance. St. Augustine, by the way, shows by numerous references (chiefly, however, to the philosophical works) that he was a close student of Apuleius, whom he claims, with manifest pride, as his countryman.

There is extant a Greek novel entitled *Lucius,* or *The Ass,* which has been commonly attributed to Apuleius' contemporary Lucian. It is very much shorter than the *Golden Ass,* perhaps less than one-eighth of its length, but presents the same story in most of the essentials. Here and there one finds, allowing for the difference of language, even verbal identity. Evidently, therefore, either Apuleius borrowed from Lucian (if he was the author) or Lucian borrowed from Apuleius, or both borrowed from some third writer. Probably both Apuleius and Lucian (or the pseudo-Lucian) derived the story of the metamorphosis and adventures of Lucius from a common source, namely a romance, no longer extant, by Lucius of Patrae. It may be accepted as certain, however, that Apuleius, while taking the outline from his Greek predecessor, added a great mass of detail, of which part was drawn from other sources but much was of his own invention. Whatever he may have borrowed, in his manner of telling the story he is wholly and magnificently original. Even in the absence of his Greek model, this, I think, will not be disputed by any one who reads the *Golden Ass* itself attentively and compares it, on the one hand with the Lucianic *Ass*, and, on the other hand, with the Apuleius revealed in the *Apologia*.

There is some reason to believe that Apuleius published the *Golden Ass* anonymously, and an ingenious critic has suggested that he may have done so because he feared that the officially virtuous Rome of Antoninus Pius, in which he was then a stranger trying to make his way at the bar, would look with disapproval upon its occasional ribaldries. Ingenious, but unconvincing. A very few years later Apuleius himself, quite as a matter of course, quotes, or rather misquotes, an extremely frank expression from one of these ribaldries when he is being tried on a grave charge before the governor of Africa: clear proof, surely, that he saw no reason to feel shame or to fear censure.[1]

Whether or not the *Golden Ass* was published anonymously, there is not the slightest doubt that Apuleius was the author. The passage in the *Apologia* to which I have just referred might itself be accepted as sufficient proof; but apart from other evidence, the language and style are conclusive. Apuleius' Latin, in its sum, is entirely his own: a Latin never written, much less spoken, by mortal man besides: a Latin compounded of the most heterogeneous elements, ancient and modern, literary and vulgar, all blended with such art, that the inconceivable miracle is wrought and there emerges from the medley a style exotic, it is true, but harmonious and extraordinarily well adapted both to the needs of the romance and to the peculiar genius of the writer. That it is a difficult Latin, follows inevitably.

But those who shrink from a work written 'in so darke

[1] *Apologia*, 33 *ad fin.*, referring to *Metamorphoses*, ii. 17.

and highe a stile, in so strange and absurde woordes, and in such newe invented phrases', have at their disposal a translation which is worthy to rank with the original itself. William Adlington's *Golden Asse*, from the preface to which I have just quoted, was first published in 1566. Those who want an accurate version to help them with the unfamiliar Latin will not go to Adlington: not even to the revised[1] Adlington printed opposite the Latin in the Loeb Classical Library. When Adlington did not know the meaning of a word or phrase, as happened often, he either made a guess or, more frequently, consulted the French and Spanish translators. Where he missed the drift of a sentence, he wrote, at any rate, something that Apuleius would not have condemned. If Apuleius, as he says, had 'suche a franke and flourishing stile, as he seemed to have the Muses alwaies at will, to feede and maineteine his penne', the same is equally true of himself. He imported into his version a quality that is essentially of his own time and race, and to that extent did not accurately mirror his original; but working in a congenial medium and on material not alien from the romantic spirit of his age, he produced a masterpiece which Apuleius, reincarnate in the age of Elizabeth, would have been glad to acknowledge as his own. Apuleius, however, would have been vastly surprised could he have had foreknowledge of the interpretation that Adlington would put upon his romance. For to Adlington the *Golden Ass* seems to subserve the ends of morality. In his preface he writes:[2] 'I trust if my simple translation be nothing accepted, yet the matter it selfe, shalbe

[1] By Sir Stephen Gaselee.

[2] My quotations of Adlington are all from the first edition. The current reprints, made from later editions, exhibit some variants from the original text.

esteemed by such, as not onely delight to please their fancie in readinge the same, but also take a pattern thereby, to regenerate their mindes from brutish and beastly custome.' And when, making a virtue of necessity, he has apologized for not offering a literal rendering, which 'in our vulgar tongue would have appeared very obscure and darke, and thereby consequently, lothsome to the Reader', he concludes: 'But how so ever it be (gentle Reader) I pray thee take it in good part, considering that for thee I have taken this paine, to the intent, that thou maist Reade the same with pleasure.'

Adlington's 'paine' gave so much pleasure that his book enjoyed a great vogue and was five times reprinted between 1566 and 1639. The edition of 1639, and some at least of the earlier reprints too, lacked not only the table of contents but also the analysis and the moral annotations with which Adlington enriched the margins of his first edition. Apuleius tells how the ass was maltreated by a niggardly and harsh mistress: 'Unhappy is he that hath an ill mistris', exclaims Adlington in the margin: 'Such scrapinge dames be many now a daies.' 'Pleasure oftentimes turneth to paine' is his comment when the horses resent the ass's intrusion into their field. The bridegroom Tlepolemus is treacherously slain: 'O wicked deede', cries Adlington, 'O more mischevous facte. Worse then Judas.' But he presently adds: 'Murder is alwaies reveled; the Goddes suffereth no vice unpunished.' To think that these pearls were cast before humourless, uncomprehending swine who did not deem them worth the reprinting!

The *Golden Ass* is divided into eleven books, but is no longer than the ordinary bookstall novel of the present day. The story, narrated by the hero Lucius himself, is as follows:

A distinguished citizen of Corinth, named Lucius, travels through Thessaly to the town of Hypata, where he becomes the guest of Milo and his wife Pamphile. Milo is a wealthy miser, and Pamphile is a practitioner of magic who is said to pay special attention to handsome young men. Lucius' curiosity is aroused. Making love to Fotis, the pretty maid-of-all-work, he persuades her to let him spy on her mistress. Pamphile, by rubbing herself with an unguent, changes herself into an owl and flies away in the night to visit her young lover. Lucius would also be transformed into a bird; but Fotis, through inadvertence, gives him the wrong unguent, so that he becomes an ass. For his comfort, Fotis assures him that if he will eat some roses he will recover human shape. Meanwhile he is happy in the discovery that, although he has the body of an ass, he has retained his human understanding; but he does not suspect that a meal of roses will be so hard to come by.

Since Lucius, the ass, cannot very well remain in the house, he goes off for the night to the stable, where he has the mortification of being kicked unmercifully by his own horse, who thinks that he has designs on the hay. Later in the night, robbers break in and lead him off with them. Heavily laden, and sorely beaten, he at last arrives with them at their cave in the mountains, where an ancient hag keeps house for them. The robbers bring in a beautiful girl, named Charite, whom they had seized and carried away on the eve of her marriage. To comfort her, the old, half-tipsy housekeeper tells her the charming fairy-tale of *Cupid and Psyche*, to the boundless admiration of the ass.

Lucius escapes with the girl on his back, but is overtaken, brought back, and punished. Charite's lover, Tlepolemus, disguised as a bloodthirsty brigand, now arrives, makes the robbers drunk, ties them up, and marches off with Charite and Lucius. When the rescue has been thus accomplished, the robbers are all killed.

The ass is now turned out to enjoy a life of ease on a farm. But here his troubles begin anew. He is overworked, and belaboured with devilish cruelty. Presently he is stolen and sold to another master. He becomes the property, in turn, of some itinerant Oriental priests, a miller, a gardener, and a soldier. But his luck was always out, until he was bought from the soldier by two brothers who were respectively pastry-cook and chef to a rich man. The ass now begins to enjoy himself hugely. Though ass in body, he retains all his fondness for human fare, and privily gorges himself with the dainties prepared by his two masters, each of whom suspects the other of shameless thieving. At last the men caught the ass in the act, and understood why he had become so wonderfully sleek. They told the story of this remarkable donkey to their master, who bought him of the brothers and handed him over to a freedman. The freedman then taught him a number of tricks for the entertainment of his patron's friends. Lucius' new owner brought him to Corinth, and arranged for him to participate in a horrible public spectacle. But when this was about to begin, Lucius broke away and fled across the Isthmus to Cenchreae, where he fell asleep on the shore. Awaking at midnight and seeing the full moon in the sky, he prayed to the Moon-goddess to restore him to human form. He then slept again; and while he slept the goddess Isis appeared to him and promised him release, stipulating that in return for her grace he should dedicate the rest of his life to her. The next day the great procession in honour of Isis came out from Corinth. The high-priest held a chaplet of roses in his hand. The ass, joining in the procession, ate some of the roses and at once regained the form of man. The high-priest, praising the irresistible power of Isis, required Lucius to devote himself to her service for ever. After a time Lucius was initiated into her mysteries, and then went to Rome where he frequented her temple. A year later, he was admitted also to the mysteries of Osiris, in which, ultimately, he attained the third degree of initiation.

This unexpected ending is clearly the invention of Apuleius himself, and may be accepted as a record of personal experience. There was in Apuleius a marked vein of mysticism and a susceptibility to religious emotion which led him, as I have said, to investigate many religions in the course of his travels and to have himself initiated into some. The worship of Isis had won countless adherents in all parts of the Roman world because it satisfied, in far larger measure than the orthodox religions of Greece and Rome, the craving of man for intimate contact with divinity. In the fulfilment of this function it was rivalled, notably, by the worship of Mithras; and these two, at first the most serious competitors with Christianity, actually helped, in the end, to prepare the way for its general acceptance. Apuleius, brought under the right influence, might easily have become a devoted Christian. But then he would never have written the *Golden Ass*.

Probably the original ending of the story was that which is preserved in the Lucianic *Ass*. There also we have the public spectacle, the escape of Lucius, the eating of roses. But thereafter the story takes quite a different turn. Lucius, on recovering his human shape, visits a lady of high degree who had shown him signal favour in his asinine days. He expects her to be no less kind now. However, the lady tells him that she much preferred him as an ass, and bids him ignominiously be gone. Had it not been clear, as I have pointed out, that Apuleius saw no reason to feel shame for his romance, one might have thought it possible that, as has been suggested, the new ending was offered by a troubled conscience as an antidote to the earlier ribaldries. Whatever Apuleius' motive in making the substitution, the new ending, though artistically inferior to the old, is of very great interest as a genuine record of religious experience.

Let me now indicate some characteristics of the romance.

The opening is excellently contrived. After a short preface we find ourselves up in the Thessalian mountains. Lucius, mounted on a white horse, has been pushing on towards Hypata, up hill and down dale, across the dew of meadows and the clods of fields. To rest his horse and stretch his legs after weary hours in the saddle, he presently dismounts, 'makes much' of his horse, removes the bit, and then proceeds slowly afoot while the animal beside him gets an 'ambulatory breakfast' by putting down its head and wrenching tufts of grass from the roadside. And so he overtakes two travelling companions who had ridden a little way ahead. 'Thessaly', the narrative begins, 'Thessaly was my destination'—and this very first word 'Thessaly', *Thessaliam*, gives the keynote of the whole romance. In all antiquity, as we learnt from the *Leucippe and Clitophon*, Thessaly is the land of witchcraft and the magic arts, a land in which, as Lucius afterwards says,[1] you believe that nothing is what it seems to be, everything has been magically transformed: the stones, the birds, the trees, the springs—all were once human; statues will walk, walls will speak, oxen will utter prophecy, from the very sky and its radiant orb will come of a sudden oracles. What manner of land it is, Lucius is soon to learn.

When Lucius has joined the other travellers he hears one of them give a great guffaw and say to his companion 'Don't tell such absurd and monstrous lies!' Hearing this, and being, as he says, always 'athirst for the new and strange'[2]— this indeed was to be his undoing—he begs a repetition of the tale which has been received with such incredulity. Whereupon Aristomenes[3] (for that was the narrator's name) tells of the grisly vengeance taken by the witch Meroe and her companion on the luckless Socrates. The tale is too long to tell in full, but here is the gist of it:

Aristomenes, a trader, came to Hypata to lay in a stock of cheese, but found that the market had been cornered by a rival. Disappointed, and wearied by a long journey, he went to the baths for refreshment. There he found his old friend Socrates, sitting on the ground in a pitiful state of

[1] ii. 1. The references here and throughout are to the Teubner edition by R. Helm.
[2] i. 2 *sititor alioquin novitatis*.
[3] Adlington, who corrupts many of Apuleius' names, calls him Aristomenus.

raggedness and squalor. Telling Socrates that at home he has been given up for dead, so that his children have been placed in the care of guardians and his wife is being urged to marry again, he takes him to his inn, gives him a wash and clothes and food and a bed, and demands an explanation of his deplorable plight. It was a long story, but amounted to this. Socrates, on his way to Larissa, had been attacked by brigands and robbed of all but the clothes that he was wearing. Making his escape, he struggled on to an inn, where he narrated his sorrowful adventures to the innkeeper, an old but still quite handsome woman named Meroe, who, after giving him a dinner without payment, made him guest in bed as well as board and reduced him to his present shameful condition. Aristomenes says that he deserved all this and more for preferring a 'leathery old harlot' to home and children. Socrates cries 'Hush, hush! She is a witch and may be overhearing us'; and he reinforces his warning with tales of the awful punishments she has inflicted on those who have offended her. She changed a faithless lover into a beaver so that he might mutilate himself; she changed a rival innkeeper into a frog and put him into a great jar of his own wine, where, down among the dregs, he hoarsely croaks officious welcome to his former customers. Even more dreadful deeds she has done to satisfy her cruel lust for revenge.

Convinced by this recital, Aristomenes proposes that they go to bed, and after a night's rest get up before daybreak and leave the town far behind them. Socrates, well plied with unaccustomed wine, falls at once into a stertorous sleep. Aristomenes bars the door, puts his bed against it, and after a while also sleeps. He was awakened by a great battering at the door, as though robbers were breaking in. Presently the door gives way, overturning the bed on top of Aristomenes, who lies on the floor like a tortoise in its shell. Peeping out, he sees two elderly women, of whom one carried a lamp and the other a sword and sponge. These were Meroe and her sister-witch Panthia. Meroe proposes vengeance on Aristomenes for his curiosity and pertness of tongue, and Panthia suggests death or mutilation. Meroe, however, decides to spare him so that he may give burial to 'this poor fellow' Socrates. The two witches then thrust the sword to the hilt through the throat and down into the body of Socrates, catch all the blood in a skin bag, take out his heart, and put the sponge in its place. Then, after befouling the terror-stricken Aristomenes, they go away.

Aristomenes now tries to escape, but is prevented by the janitor: how is the janitor to know that he is not a fugitive from justice, that he has not, for example, killed the companion who shared his lodging? So Aristomenes must perforce wait for daybreak, and actually falls into a sound sleep. Roused by the janitor, he finds Socrates already awake, and thinks that he must have dreamed it all. So off the two friends go, conversing cheerfully, and after a time halt for a meal under the trees by a river. Having eaten, Socrates goes down on his knees by the stream to drink. But as he stooped, the sponge fell out through the wound that the witch had made, a few drops of blood followed, and the lifeless body of Socrates would have fallen into the river had not Aristomenes pulled it back. Aristomenes gave the body scant burial, and fled as though he were the murderer of his friend.

'This tale' (I quote from Adlington)—'This tale tolde Aristomenus, and his fellowe whiche before obstinately would give no credite unto him, began to say: Verely there was never so foolish a tale, nor a more absurde lie tolde then this: and then he spake unto me, saiyng: Ho sir, what you are I know not, but youre habite and countenance declareth, that you should be some honest gentleman, do you beleeve his tale? yea verely (quoth I) why not? for what so ever the fates hath apointed to men, that I beleeve shall happen. For many thinges chaunce unto me, and unto you, and to divers others, which beinge declared unto the ignorant be accompted as lies. But verely I give credite unto his tale, and render entier thankes unto him in that (by the pleasant relation thereof) we have quickly passed and shortned our journey, and I thinke that my horse also was delighted with the same, and hath brought me to the gate of this Citie without any paine at all.'

There you have the true spirit of the story-teller, the spirit in which this wonder-tale of transformation is told, the spirit in which the reader, too, should approach any work of fiction. What matter whether the tale be true or false? Let the reader give thanks to the teller for his 'pleasant relation'.

The story of Meroe and Socrates illustrates very well that taste for gruesome tales of mystery and witchcraft, in which Apuleius does not yield place even to Poe. One can imagine Apuleius saying to his readers, in anticipation of the Fat Boy, 'I wants to make your flesh creep.' And creep it does. Do you thrill to a ghost story? Have you a liking for the macabre? Then read, in the second book of the *Golden Ass*, how Thelyphron[1] watched over a corpse through a long night, and what befell him. Again I can give no more than an abstract.

Thelyphron ('Softy', as he is unkindly named) tells the tale after dinner at the request of his hostess. After long travels from Miletus[2] to the Olympic Games and thence through Greece, the young Thelyphron found himself in Thessaly, and in an evil hour came to Larissa.

---

[1] Adlington called him Telephoron in the narrative, Bellephoron in the chapter-heading. In the sixth edition there is yet another spelling, Bellepheron.

[2] Perhaps, then, this is one of the 'Milesian Tales', though free from the taint of obscenity.

Having run through most of his money, he went in quest of work. In the market-place he encountered an old man standing on a stone and offering payment to any one who would undertake to watch over a corpse. 'What is this I find?' he asked of a passer-by; 'Do the dead run away here?' 'Ah!' replied the other, 'you are young, and a stranger, and of course don't know that you are in Thessaly where witches are always nibbling the faces of the dead.' After negotiation with the old man, Thelyphron accepts the office of watcher for a fee of ten pounds, and is warned that he must guard carefully 'from the wicked Harpies' the body of the son of a noble house. 'Stuff and nonsense!' he replies; 'you see a man of iron, sleepless, all eyes.'

He now comes to the house of mourning and is brought into the chamber where the body lies. In the presence of seven witnesses he is bidden to note that nose and eyes and ears and lips and chin are all whole; and having done so, asks for a large lamp, a good supply of wine, and a tray of food. All of these, except the lamp, the weeping matron who is his conductress refuses indignantly. 'Do you think', she asks him, 'that you have come here to hold revel?' And thereupon she orders a maid to give him lamp and oil, lock him in, and be gone. So the long watch began. Thelyphron, left alone, rubbed his eyes and 'armed them for wakefulness' and sang to keep up his spirits. Twilight came, and then night; and as the weary hours of night wore on, he grew more and more oppressed with the weight of fear. Then of a sudden a weasel crept in and stood before him and stared sharply at him, so that the great boldness of the tiny creature made him sorely afraid. 'Be off,' he cried, 'foul beast! Back to your rattish kind, before you feel my strength! Be off!' And when the weasel had run out of the room Thelyphron forthwith fell into so profound a sleep that Apollo himself could not have told which was the more dead, he or the corpse.

Day came, and Thelyphron, jingling his golden fee and proffering future service, went his way. Presently he fell in with the funeral procession of the man whom he had guarded, as it passed through the market-place. An old man, garbed as a mourner and weeping and tearing his hair, cried out that the dead man, his nephew, had been poisoned by his adulterous wife. He demanded vengeance. In the riot that ensued, the woman denied her guilt. Thereupon the old man produced an Egyptian magician who with herb and prayer recalled the dead man 'from draughts of Lethe and the pools of Styx' back to momentary life. Thus revived, the victim confirmed the charge, which the woman, however, continued to deny. Then he proceeded to proof of his truthfulness. With much circumstantial detail, he told how during the vigil the witches cast the watcher into a deathlike sleep. Now the dead man, as it chanced, also bore the name Thelyphron, and when the witches called him it was Thelyphron the sleeper, not Thelyphron the dead, who came to them. From him they cut off nose and ears, replacing them with wax: 'there he is now, poor fellow, with mutilation as reward of his diligence!' Poor Thelyphron, terrified by what he had heard, caught hold of his nose: it came away; he rubbed his ears, and they fell off. And so while the bystanders bubbled with laughter, he slunk away.

Among the merits of this story is the characterization of the unfortunate Thelyphron. There is no formal description of him, and yet one sees him so very clearly: a well-meaning but cocksure fellow, honest but blundering: as when, on completing his watch over the corpse and receiving his fee, he begs the widow to hold him entirely at her service the next time she has a corpse to mind. But throughout the work Apuleius displays an excellence in character-drawing that is possible only to an acute observer of human nature and a master of language. As in the *Satiricon*, so also in the *Golden Ass*, we find no puppets, but living men and women.

Consider, for instance, Pythias, in the first book, portrayed with the quiet humour that is characteristic of our author. Lucius, knowing that he will fare poorly if he relies on his miserly host's table, goes to the market and, after some haggling about the price, buys fish for his supper. As he was leaving the market, he encountered his old school-friend Pythias. 'I pray you tell me,' he said, 'what meaneth these servitours that follow you, and these roddes . . . which they beare: and this habite whiche you weare, like unto a Magistrate.' Pythias is immensely pleased at this recognition of his dignity and is determined to impress his friend still more deeply. Adlington's version does not bring out the full flavour of Pythias's reply, with its pompously deprecatory 'plurals of modesty'—'*annonam curamus*', *ait*, '*et aedilem gerimus*', and so forth—but it will serve. 'I beare the office and rule of the clarke of the market,' he says, 'and therefore if you will have any pittance for your supper, speake and I will purvey it for you.' Lucius explained that he had already bought some fish, and mentioned the price. Pythias took the basket and marched up to the fishmonger in fine indignation. 'Is it thus that you serve and handle straungers? . . .

wherefore sell you this fishe so deere which is not woorth a halfpennie? . . . Assure your selfe that you shall not escape without punishment, and you shal know what mine office is, and how I ought to punish such as doo offend.' And then, says Lucius, 'he toke my basket and cast the fishe on the grounde, and commaunded one of his sergeantes to treade them under his feete: this done he perswaded me to departe, and said that that onely shame and reproche done unto the olde caitife did suffise him, so I went away all amased and astonied, towardes the baines . . . where when I had washed and refreshed my bodie, I returned againe to Milos house both without money and meate'.

Fotis, the pretty, roguish, affectionate maidservant of Milo, with whom Lucius falls in love, and who is the innocent cause of his transformation into an ass, is delineated by Apuleius with consummate art. A comparison with the corresponding chapters of the Lucianic *Ass* indicates how vastly Apuleius must have improved on his Greek original. An epithet here, a simple utterance there, and you have her to the life. When he contemplates the charms of her person, he breaks into rhapsody. Lucius, a connoisseur of female beauty, comes upon Fotis in the kitchen,[1] daintily dressed in linen frock and red sash, stirring a dish with circular movement of her blossom-like open hands, and swaying gracefully to the rhythm of her beat. Lucius stood astonished at her loveliness. Then follows a 'purple patch' on which our novelist-rhetorician has expended all his art. Thus Adlington:

'Whatsoever flourishyng and gorgeous apparell doth worke and set foorth in the corporal partes of a woman,

[1] ii. 7 ff.

the same doth the naturall and comely beautie set out in the face. Moreover there be divers, that (to the intent to showe their grace and feauture) will cast of their partlettes, collars, habillimentes, frontes, cornettes and krippins, and doo more delight to showe the fairenes of their skinne, then to decke them selves up in golde and pretious stone. But because it is a crime unto me to say so, and to give no example thereof, know ye: that if you spoile and cut of the heare of any woman or deprive her of the colour of her face, though she weare never so excellent in beautie, though she weare throwen downe from heaven, spronge of the seas, nourished of the floudes, though she weare Venus her selfe, though she weare accompanied with the Graces, though she weare wayted upon of all the courte of Cupide, though she weare girded with her beautifull skarfe of love, and though she smelled of perfumes and muskes, yet if she appered balde: she coulde in no wise please, no, not her owne Vulcanus. O how well doth a fayre colour, and a shininge face agree with glitteringe heare? Beholde it encountereth with the beames of the sunne, and pleaseth the eie mervelously. Sometimes the beautie of the heare resembleth the colour of Golde and honie, sometimes the blewe plume and asured feathers about the neckes of dooves, especially when it is either annoincted with the gumme of Arabia, or trimlie tufte out with the teeth of a fine combe, whiche if it be tied up in the pole of the necke, it seemeth to the lover (that beholdeth the same) as a glasse that yeldeth foorth a more pleasant and gratious comelines then if it shoulde be sparsed abroade on the shoulders of the woman or hange downe scatteringe behinde. Finally, there is suche a dignitie in the heare, that what so ever she be, though she never be so bravely attired with golde, silkes, pretious stones, and other riche and gorgeous ornamentes, yet if her heare be not curiously set foorth, she cannot seeme faire.'

This passage, even in Adlington's far from literal translation, well exemplifies the opulence of vocabulary and the elaborate felicity—*curiosa felicitas*—of diction which Apuleius had so completely at command. Apuleius had an observant and appreciative eye for physical details, and a faculty for the description of them which has rarely been excelled. His luxuriant senses were titillated by bright colours and sweet odours and graceful forms, and he loved to translate these into language as sensuous as his emotions. But the most notable examples of this are to be found in the *Cupid and Psyche*.

The whole work abounds in humour. Sometimes, it must be confessed, though not often, the humour is of that deplorable kind which turns upon the misfortune of others, as when the guests at Byrrhena's dinner-party find something vastly amusing in the mutilation of poor Thelyphron, or the crowd in the theatre is consumed with mirth while Lucius is being tried for his life. This second story, like the first, is admirably told.[1] Lucius, returning from dinner late at night and 'well tippled', found three gigantic burglars breaking into his host's house. He gave battle and killed them. Next day he was arrested and charged with murdering three inoffensive citizens. The trial took place in the theatre before a huge and jeering crowd. In his defence, Lucius relates what the leader of the gang said to his companions; how one of the robbers struck him with a stone, the second bit him, the third ran at him. He slew them all. It was the perfect defence of justifiable homicide, but court and spectators, even his host Milo, dissolved in laughter. Instruments of torture were brought in, and as a last refinement of cruelty Lucius was commanded to uncover the bodies of his victims.

[1] ii. 32 to iii. 10.

'But ye gracious gods,' he exclaims, 'what a sight was there!.... Those bodies of slain men were three inflated skins pierced with holes and, as I recalled my battle of the evening before, gaping in the places where I had wounded the robbers.' 'Whereat' (I now quote from Adlington) 'the people laughed exceedingely. Some rejoysed mervelously with the remembraunce thereof, some helde their stomakes that aked with joye, but every man delighted at this passyng sporte, and so departed out of the Theatre.'—Lucius had been the victim of a practical joke, chosen for sacrifice at the annual festival of Laughter. It was from this episode in the *Golden Ass* that Cervantes derived the incident of Don Quixote and the wineskins.

In the story about the joke played upon Lucius, and still more in the story about the mutilation of Thelyphron, the humour is marred by an element of cruelty; but in Apuleius such lapses are rare. Soon after his trial, Lucius, having essayed the great adventure, is changed into an ass, and Apuleius gives free rein to his humour in relating his hero's experiences. Apuleius knows exactly what it must feel like to be an ass, and yet to be conscious of humanity. Lucius does his best to walk humbly, to behave as a good ass should. Sometimes, however, he is moved to revolt. When he is being led, overladen and weary, aching and footsore, bullied and beaten, to the robbers' den in the mountains, he resolves to lie down and refuse to budge, even at the risk of a flogging.[1] But the other ass anticipates him and is killed, most horribly, for his pains. Thereupon Lucius 'purposed now to forgette al subtiltie and deceite, and to play the good Asse to gette (his) Maisters

[1] iv. 4-5.

favour'. A very ass, you see, but a wise ass. And how
pathetic a figure he is when some robbers come in and
relate how they are now safe from accusation because
Lucius, having disappeared from Milo's house on the
night of the robbery, has been charged with the crime![1]
In his indignation at this monstrous charge, he wanted
to cry *non feci*! 'I didn't do it!' But though he rounded
his great pendulous lips and did his best, he could get
no further than *non, non*: poor ass, his assy lips could
achieve no more. He is a good-hearted ass, too. How
he weeps when he hears the sobs of poor little Charite,
ravished away by the robbers on the eve of her wedding![2] And he is a virtuous ass—if not always in his
own conduct, at any rate in his judgements on the conduct of others. He had thought Charite a dear, good
little maid; and when he finds her cheerful and smiling
at Tlepolemus' suggestion to the robbers that she be
sold to some trafficker in vice (this, of course, is part of
Tlepolemus' plan to rescue her from her captors), he
is horrified. 'I thought evil', he says, 'of the whole sex.
. . . And at that time all the tribe of women and their
morals depended on the judgment of an ass.'[3]

To the food that is proper for asses Lucius never became thoroughly reconciled, as he several times reminds
us. He tells us how, for instance, when a party of robbers returned with rich plunder, the old housekeeper
served out unlimited barley to him and the horse. The
horse thought he was enjoying *Saliares cenas*, an alder-
manic feast; but the ass, having spied out a nook where
there was a great pile of loaves, made a hearty meal of
them: 'I exercise valiantly', he says, 'a gullet that was
all flabby and cobwebbed with long starvation.'[4]

[1] vii. 1–3.   [2] iv. 24.   [3] vii. 10.   [4] iv. 22.

Lucius, the ass, acknowledges moments of pride, also, as when he realizes how artistically he is telling his tale. Thus in the sixth chapter of Book IV: 'The thing and the time compelleth me to make description of the places, and specially of the denne where the theeves did inhabite, I wil prove my witte what I can doo, and then consider you whether I was an Asse in judgement and sense, or no.' And he proves his judgement and sense by a masterly description of a real robbers' den in the mountains, and of real robbers in it: not such animated sticks as you will meet in the Greek novels, for example in *Leucippe and Clitophon*. Apuleius' brigands are as life-like as Stevenson's pirates. They bear names of awe: Alcimus the stout-hearted; Thrasyleon bold as a lion; Lamachus doughty in battle. Great lusty fellows they are, not without courage, exhibiting a touch of sardonic humour, cruel to the point of ruthlessness. But their brawn is superior to their brain. Like the Sons of Gama in *Princess Ida*,

> On the whole (they) are
> Not intelligent:
> No, no, no,
> Not intelligent.

Read, for instance, in Book IV,[1] the tale of the robber Alcimus, who broke into a room where an old woman lay asleep, and proceeded to throw its contents, including the bedclothes, out of the window to his comrades below. The old lady, awakened, begged him not to bestow her poor possessions on her neighbours, who were too rich to need them. Alcimus went to the window to have a look. Then 'the old woman marked him well, and came behinde him softlie, and although she

[1] iv. 12.

had but small strength, yet with a sodaine force she tooke him by the heeles and thrust him out headlonge, and so he fell upon a mervelous great stone, and burst his ribbes, whereby he vomited and spued flakes of bloud, and presently died: Then,' continues the narrator, 'we threw him into the river likewise, as we had done Lamathus[1] before: When we had thus lost twoo of our compaignions, we liked not Thebes, but marched towardes the next Citie called Platea.'

When Lucius has at last escaped from the robbers, his troubles are by no means at an end. Bought and sold, lost and found, carrying loads, turning a mill, sorely beaten, threatened with maiming and death, on he passes through mountains and forests, fields and towns, bearing many hardships and cruelties with pathetic resignation, rarely provoked to retaliate on a persecutor, until in the hands of his last owners he finds relief from his sufferings in a life of ease and luxury. Presently came release from the assy shape, and then, as one might say, a magnificent revenge. For this much-enduring ass was also an ass of high intelligence, observant of eye and receptive of ear; indeed, his one comfort in his assy deformity, he tells us,[2] was the exceedingly long and serviceable pair of ears with which Fotis's error had endowed him; and he has included in the chronicle of his adventures such a recital of the follies and villainies that he saw and heard, that their authors are exposed to the mockery and censure of all posterity!

For in the *Golden Ass*, apart from the main story, there are many *novelle*, excellently told and ingeniously incorporated. It is no longer possible to determine which of

---

[1] So Adlington calls Lamachus.   [2] ix. 15.

these Apuleius borrowed and which he invented. In his preface he indicates that some, at least, are of the kind known as Milesian Tales, of which, as I have said, the most famous is the story of the Matron of Ephesus, first recorded by Petronius in the *Satiricon*. Two of Apuleius' stories reappear in the *Decameron*,[1] by direct derivation. But the best of all the *novelle* in the *Golden Ass* is the tale of *Cupid and Psyche*, which is a whole romance in itself and occupies about one-seventh of the eleven books. It is told by the aged, bibulous housekeeper of the robbers, up in the wild mountains of Thessaly, to cheer Charite the ravished bride. A strange but effective setting for so dainty and brilliant a gem!

The tale begins in the traditional manner of the fairy-story: *Erant in quadam civitate rex et regina*, 'Once upon a time there were a king and a queen'. These had three very beautiful daughters. But whereas the two elder daughters were of merely mortal beauty, the youngest, whose name was Psyche, was of such surpassing loveliness that people came flocking from far and near to marvel at her, and worshipped her as a goddess. And so it came to pass that Venus was forgotten, and plotted revenge. Psyche's father was commanded by an oracle to leave her on the edge of a cliff, arrayed as for a bridal of death. She would receive a bridegroom, not of mortal stock, but cruel and venomous: a winged monster before whom Jove himself trembled. When Psyche was thus abandoned, Zephyr, the mild west-wind, came, wafted her from the cliff, and brought her gently to rest on a meadow in the valley below. Here she saw a palace of miraculous

[1] v. 10 and vii. 2, from Apuleius ix. 22 ff. and ix. 5 ff.

splendour, and went in. A bodiless voice bade her enjoy all that she saw. On a table were the daintiest of viands, mysteriously spread by invisible hands, and the air thrilled with wondrous music. Night fell, and in the darkness came the unseen bridegroom, and was gone before break of day.

The husband forbids Psyche to look upon his face and form. But against his wish, the two sisters come to the valley, and seeing all the magnificence amid which Psyche is living they are jealous. They come a second time, and a third, and try to persuade her that she is married to a loathsome serpent. They advise her to kill him, and so are wafted home again. That night Psyche arose, meaning to kill her husband. But the light from her lamp showed her 'the gentlest and dearest of all monsters, the beautiful god Cupid himself'. In her joyful agitation at this discovery, she let a drop of hot oil from the lamp fall on the god's shoulder, whereat he awoke and flew away. From a cypress-top he told Psyche how Venus had commanded him to make her enamoured of some unworthy lover, and how he had fallen in love with her himself. He promises that the jealous sisters, who have wrought the present mischief, shall suffer condign punishment: Psyche herself he will punish only by his flight from her.

Psyche must now leave the happy valley and wander over the world in search of Cupid, enduring the while many woes. The rest of the story relates how the jealous sisters were dashed to death from the cliff; how Psyche, in her despair, dared to appeal to Venus herself, but was beaten cruelly and made to perform difficult and dangerous tasks, in which she was helped by the lowly things of earth. Her final task was to visit Proserpine

in the underworld and bring back to Venus in a casket
some part of Proserpine's beauty. She accomplished
the perilous journey; but when returning she yielded
to her curiosity and opened the casket. Out came
Sleep, the brother of Death, and Psyche fell lifeless.
But Cupid, now healed of his burn, hastened to her.
He woke her with a prick of his arrow, and Psyche
carried the casket to Venus.

All ends happily. Jove, on the intercession of Cupid,
convenes an assembly of the gods, before which he formally announces the marriage of Cupid and Psyche.
On Psyche he confers immortality. And when the time
was come, Psyche bore to Cupid a daughter, whose
name was Voluptas.

Adlington's version of this story has the merits to be
found in the rest of his work; but the essential qualities
of the *Cupid and Psyche* are more clearly mirrored in the
epitome of the tale which Walter Pater has included in
Marius the Epicurean. Here is a specimen. Psyche has
been wafted down into the valley:

'Psyche, in those delicate grassy places, lying sweetly on
her dewy bed, rested from the agitation of her soul and arose
in peace. And lo! a grove of mighty trees, with a fount of
water, clear as glass, in the midst; and hard by the water,
a dwelling-place, built not by human hands but by some
divine cunning. One recognised, even at the entering, the
delightful hostelry of a god. Golden pillars sustained the
roof, arched most curiously in cedar-wood and ivory. The
walls were hidden under wrought silver:—all tame and
woodland creatures leaping forward to the visitor's gaze.
Wonderful indeed was the craftsman, divine or half-divine,
who by the subtlety of his art had breathed so wild a soul

into the silver! The very pavement was distinct with pictures in goodly stones. In the glow of its precious metal the house is its own daylight, having no need of the sun. Well might it seem a place fashioned for the conversation of gods with men!

'Psyche, drawn forward by the delight of it, came near, and, her courage growing, stood within the doorway. One by one, she admired the beautiful things she saw; and, most wonderful of all! no lock, no chain, nor living guardian protected that great treasure house. But as she gazed there came a voice—a voice, as it were unclothed of bodily vesture —"Mistress!" it said, "all these things are thine." . . . And Psyche understood that some divine care was providing, and, refreshed with sleep and the Bath, sat down to the feast. Still she saw no one: only she heard words falling here and there, and had voices alone to serve her. And the feast being ended, one entered the chamber and sang to her unseen, while another struck the chords of a harp, invisible with him who played on it. Afterwards the sound of a company singing together came to her, but still so that none were present to sight; yet it appeared that a great multitude of singers was there.'

Now that, as all will agree, is very beautifully done, and it reproduces faithfully the manner and the tone both of the passage which it represents and of much else in the *Cupid and Psyche*. But not all is so satisfactory. Pater, being Pater, is delicate where delicacy is not; and he has consciously[1] transposed the more frivolous parts of his original into a graver key.

Psyche is the most charming and lovable of fairy princesses; a maid of divine beauty, an affectionate daughter, brave at need to face death itself, simple and childlike in her enjoyment of the wonders of her valley,

[1] *Marius the Epicurean*, Part I, ch. 6.

devoted to the husband who comes to her so miraculously; yet withal not altogether free from human frailty. When her trustfulness is betrayed by the envious sisters, she is relentless in vengeance. In time of need, like the other heroines of the ancient romances, she is not above telling a fib or two. She has full measure of that foible which man calls feminine, an insatiable curiosity. Twice this curiosity was her undoing: once, when she took the lamp to look upon her husband; a second time, when she yielded to the temptation of opening Proserpine's casket. 'See, how silly I am,' she says,[1] 'who, bearing the divine beauty, take not the least little bit from it for myself, or thus to please my lover, my beautiful!' So she opened the casket; and within was not the divine cosmetic, but sleep as of the dead.

How pathetic a figure she is in the days of her thraldom to Venus, when, lonely and oppressed, yet hoping to win her way in the end to her beloved, she goes about the cruel tasks that Venus has imposed on her! Pathetic, yet drawing to herself, unasked, the sympathy of lowly creatures. Thus she is helped by the tiny ants, nimble fosterlings of Earth the All-Mother;[2] by the green reed, dear sweet nursing-mother of music.[3] And the eagle, royal bird of Jupiter most high, goes in her stead when, though the very streams take voice and warn her of deadly peril, she would venture, at Venus' command, among the unsleeping dragons that infest the tumbling waters of Styx.[4]

So much, then, for Psyche. Cupid, her lover and

---

[1] vi. 20.
[2] vi. 10 *terrae omniparentis agiles alumnae*: Pater quaintly renders *alumnae* 'scholars'.
[3] vi. 12 *musicae suavis nutricula*.   [4] vi. 14–15.

bridegroom, is not the grave and even terrible young god imagined of poets and sculptors in Greece's prime, but the wayward, winged archer-boy of the Alexandrians. Apuleius introduces him thus:[1]

'And without more ado Venus calls that winged and most audacious boy of hers, who, rogue that he is, scorns the morality of the state. For he goes armed with flames and arrows, runs about through other people's houses by night spoiling everybody's marriage, suffers no punishment for such outrageous conduct, and in fact does nothing good at all. And though his native lawlessness makes him froward, she actually incites him to mischief besides, and takes him to that city and points out Psyche to him', and entreats him, as he loves his mother, to punish severely the girl's 'contumacious beauty'.

Apollo, the cold-blooded bachelor, has not a good word to say for him: in the oracle given to Psyche's father he calls Cupid a 'cruel, wild, evil serpent-thing'.[2] What Jove himself thought of Cupid appears when Cupid comes to him as a suppliant.[3] One may translate the passage thus:

'Then Jupiter pinched Cupid's chubby cheek and kissed his hand and said to him: "Though you, sir son, have never shown me the respect decreed to me by grace of the gods, but have pierced with wound on wound this breast of mine that hath the disposition of the elements and the changing stars; and though, time after time, you have disgraced me with an earthly passion, and, contrary to the laws—even the Julian law—and to public morality, have injured my reputation and good name with shameful amours, sordidly changing my serene features into serpents and fires and beasts and birds and cattle of the pastures; nevertheless,

[1] iv. 30.   [2] iv. 33 *saevum atque ferum vipereumque malum.*   [3] vi. 22.

mindful of my moderation, and remembering that these hands of mine have had your upbringing, I'll do all that you ask—provided only that you know how to beware of your rivals, and that if there happens to be at present any particularly prepossessing piece of femininity on earth,[1] you remember that you must make her my recompense for this service." '

Cupid had been a very naughty boy, just as his grand-father Jupiter was still a very naughty old gentleman. His mother Venus, as Purser observes,[2] did not realize that he was now grown up, or she would never have commissioned him to punish an extremely pretty girl. Of course Cupid fell in love with Psyche, and became at once a model husband. The phenomenon has been repeated often enough since Cupid vanished with the rest of the Olympians.

We have just seen what Apuleius makes of Jupiter. He is equally disrespectful in his treatment of other divinities, rivalling in his mockery Lucian himself. What a termagant he makes of Venus! Venus was far away, bathing in the Ocean,[3] when the white seamew, a chattering fowl, flew to her and told her that Cupid was spending his time in dalliance. This was bad enough, even if, as Venus supposed, the boy had yielded to the blandishments of some Nymph or Hour or Muse; but when she is told that the hussy is a girl whose name, if the bird remembers it aright, is Psyche, and realizes that it was herself who brought them to-gether, she is furious. And so when poor Psyche, sick at heart and ailing in body, comes to Venus' court,[4] hoping against hope for mercy, she receives no gracious

---

[1] *si qua nunc in terris punlla praepollet pulchritudine.*
[2] *Cupid and Psyche*, ed. L. C. Purser, p. lix.
[3] v. 28.
[4] vi. 8–10.

welcome but is dragged by the hair into the presence. Then

'As soon as Venus saw her she gave a great loud laugh of fury; and shaking her head and scratching her right ear, she cried: "So at last you have seen fit to call on your mother-in-law! Or perhaps you have come to see your husband whom you have wounded dangerously? Oh, you need not be alarmed; I'll welcome you like a nice good daughter-in-law." ' And she called in her handmaids Anxiety and Sorrow, who, at her command, took Psyche and flogged her and tortured her and brought her back to their mistress. Then Venus laughed again and said: "And look! she thinks to move me to pity by her expectations: I'm to be made the happy grandmother of a fine bouncing baby, please you! It will be pleasant for me, won't it, to be called grandmother in my prime, pleasant that the son of a good-for-nothing servant-girl shall be called the grandson of Venus!" '

And after plainly suggesting that Psyche has not her marriage-lines and that the child will be a bastard, Venus flew at her, ripped her dress to rags, tore her hair, and knocked her down. And the rest of her conduct is of a piece with this, except that at the end she is mollified enough to dance at the wedding.

Mercury, the herald of the gods, is turned into an ordinary town-crier, as we shall see presently. Ceres, when Psyche appeals to her,[1] proves to be amiable but weak. She is on friendly terms with her kinswoman Venus—a thoroughly respectable woman, too—and cannot risk offending her; her conscience, evidently, is not at ease, but she salves it by virtuously abstaining from the arrest of the fugitive. In Juno, also, to whom

[1] vi. 2–3.

Psyche next applies for aid,[1] family loyalties are too strong. Nothing would give her greater pleasure than to grant Psyche's prayer; but really, against the will of Venus, her son's wife, whom she has loved as a daughter —well, it would be hardly decent. And besides, think of the laws that forbid the harbouring of other people's runaway slaves! How *could* she?

Of the deities, only Pan,[2] dear old rustic Pan, is treated with respect. Psyche comes upon him where he sits on a rise above a stream, combining a little love-making with a music lesson. He is only a rough old fellow, he says, but in his long life has had a deal of experience; and he pauses from his agreeable occupations to tell her what a dear, pretty girl she is, and to offer sympathy and good advice.

If Apuleius does not make his gods and goddesses conspicuously divine, at least he makes them most realistically human. Of the mortals, the two sisters of Psyche are excellently portrayed. So are their husbands, who, though they do not appear in person, are described for dramatic purposes by their respective wives.[3] The sisters have returned home after seeing the splendours of Psyche's palace and being told, mendaciously, that she is married to a godlike young man who is not there, when the sisters call, because he spends most of his time out hunting. 'Just see', says one of them, 'how blind and cruel and unjust is Fortune! . . . And if Psyche also has this marvellously handsome husband that she talks about, she is the luckiest woman in the whole world. . . . But I, poor woman, have drawn[4] a husband who is older than my father: a bald-headed

---

[1] vi. 4.　　　　　　[2] v. 25.　　　　　　[3] v. 9-10.
[4] *sortita sum*, as in a matrimonial lottery.

pumpkin-pate, feebler than any chit of a child, who keeps the whole house shut up and bolted and barred.'[1] And the other rejoins: 'Yes, and I have to put up with a husband who besides is so bent and doubled up with rheumatism that he hardly ever gives a thought to me. I spend most of my time rubbing his twisted and calcified fingers, chafing these hands of mine, these delicate hands, with stinking fomentations and dirty rags and noisome plasters, not looking like a dutiful wife, but playing the part of a hard-worked lady doctor.'

Walter Pater, in the criticism which precedes his paraphrase of the *Cupid and Psyche*, says that you might, if you chose, take this charming tale as an allegory. Many have done so: they have interpreted Cupid as Love, Psyche as the Soul, and the fruit of their union, Voluptas, as Pleasure. And yet, there is little to be said for this view. Indeed, on a closer inspection, the details of the story seem almost to exclude it. The names of hero and heroine may have been suggested to Apuleius by the association of Love and the Soul in Alexandrian poets, and there may well be a touch of allegory in the birth of Voluptas, Pleasure, as the daughter of Cupid and Psyche; but scarcely more than that. Psyche herself is entirely human, no mere personification of the Soul: indeed, as Purser pointed out,[2] she herself possesses a soul. The light-hearted cynicism with which Apuleius handles his divinities would be altogether out of place in an allegory: how absurdly misplaced, for instance, would be the incident of Mercury's search for Psyche and his amusing proclamation of the reward to

---

[1] Note that in her indignation she becomes bitterly alliterative.
[2] Op. cit., p. lxi, referring to v. 6 and v. 13.

be paid for her by Venus![1] Mercury travels the whole world over, looking for the girl and crying this advertisement:

'ESCAPED: a princess named Psyche, maidservant of Venus. Whosoever can bring back the runaway or show where she is hiding, is to interview the crier Mercury behind the Murcian Pillars.[2] REWARD FOR INFORMATION: seven sweet kisses, and one long, lingering honied lover's kiss, from Venus herself.'[3]

And if this were allegory, the supreme god would surely not add to his blessing of the mystic marriage of Love and the Soul such shameless references to his own peccadilloes.

No, this is not an allegory, but an old folk-tale in a new dress, a highly elaborated version of the story of Beauty and the Beast. The beautiful maiden; the wondrous palace; the unseen and unnamed husband who either is, or is said to be, a serpent; the disobedience of the wife, her ensuing sorrow and suffering; the final reconciliation;—not a detail is wanting. And this story you will find among many peoples, ancient and modern, civilized and barbarous, 'from China to Peru'.

There can be few single works of literature that have exerted as powerful and widespread an influence as the *Metamorphoses* of Apuleius, the tale of 'transformations' which we are accustomed to call the *Golden Ass*. You will find it, to mention only a few names at random, among Englishmen in Edmund Spenser and Thomas

[1] vi. 8.

[2] The *metae Murciae* were conical pillars on the Great Racecourse (*Circus Maximus*) in Rome, named after an early Roman divinity called Murcia. Evidently Apuleius was one of those who identified Murcia with Venus.

[3] Alliteration again: '*ab ipsa Venere Septem savia suavia et unum blandientis adpulsu linguae longe mellitum*'.

Heywood and John Keats and William Morris and Robert Bridges; among Italians in Boccaccio (whose manuscript of the whole romance, written by his own hand, is still extant) and Boiardo; among Spaniards in Cervantes and Calderon; among Frenchmen in La Fontaine and Fontenelle; among Germans, notably in Wieland. The *Cupid and Psyche* has inspired not only great writers, but many great painters and sculptors, including Raphael and Canova and Rodin. But the topic is too spacious for treatment here, and has received adequate attention elsewhere.[1]

If any were disposed to condemn Apuleius' romance because of its occasional frankness in dealing with human weaknesses, I should first confront them with the illustrious witnesses to its excellence whom I have just named; but I should also remind them that it has been highly regarded by men of eminence in the Christian Church, from St. Augustine to Bishop Warburton.[2] Warburton, indeed, though few would now agree with him, saw in it a parable of the brutishness of vice and the salvation that comes from religion, even if that religion be not the Christian; St. Augustine thought that it might even record the personal experience of the fellow countryman whom he so greatly admired. Men of sound judgement and decent morals will concur with St. Augustine to this extent, at least: in esteeming this *Ass* of Apuleius an Ass of Gold. I therefore repeat the exhortation and promise with which Apuleius closes his preface: *Lector, intende*: *laetaberis*—'Reader, give heed: you will enjoy yourself.'

[1] One of the most concise and convenient discussions of it will be found in Professor Elizabeth Haight's *Apuleius and his Influence* (Harrap, 1927).

[2] Reported by Dunlop, *History of Prose Fiction*, ch. ii.

INDEX